D1011647

K-POP
A TO Z

The Definitive K-Pop Encyclopedia

BINA LEE

RACEHORSE PUBLISHING

Racehorse Publishing books may be purchased in bulk at special discounts for sales promotion, corporate gifts, fund-raising, or educational purposes. Special editions can also be created to specifications. For details, contact the Special Sales Department, Racehorse Publishing, 307 West 36th Street, 11th Floor, New York, NY 10018 or info@skyhorsepublishing.com.

Racehorse Publishing™ is a pending trademark of Skyhorse Publishing, Inc.®, a Delaware corporation.
Visit our website at www.skyhorsepublishing.com.

10 9 8 7 6 5 4 3 2 1

Library of Congress Cataloging-in-Publication Data is available on file.

Print ISBN: 978-1-63158-447-3
Ebook ISBN: 978-1-63158-448-0

Printed in the United States of America

CONTENTS

PREFACE

I distinctly remember being in seventh grade when I got my first real taste of K-pop. For me, it was one of South Korea's first ever, super popular boy bands, H.O.T, and the song "Candy" that had me hooked. Simply put, I was in love! Little did I know that what I was listening to in seventh grade would remain a lifelong passion of mine. I'm so glad that I have this opportunity to share this with you through this encyclopedia! Maybe you are a longtime supporter of K-pop and want to learn more. Or quite possibly, you're a new listener and BTS's smash hit "Mic Drop" has you hooked just like H.O.T did so many years ago for me. Either way, if K-pop is your old thing or new love, this is the perfect book for you.

K-pop (케이팝) is the monster genre of the Korean culture that has gathered an enormous following both inside and outside of South Korea. Although it has been around for decades, it has grown exponentially in recent years with fans from all over the world loving and appreciating this particular aspect of South Korean culture. K-pop groups like BTS, BIGBANG, and Girls' Generation have put South Korea on the international pop-culture map. There's something about K-pop, from the cool concepts to the roles of each group member, all the way down to their amazing choreography and fashion, that we just can't seem to get enough of! This encyclopedia was designed to educate both those who are just starting to fall in love with K-pop and those who just can't seem to get enough! Regardless of which category you fit into, it's a great book to have in your collection if you're a die-hard K-pop fan. I truly hope this guide is fun to read and helps you navigate the ever-evolving K-Pop subculture that continues to take the world by storm.

A.C.E

A.C.E, which stands for "Adventure Calling Emotions," was founded under the company Beat Interactive in May of 2017. The members include Jun, Donghun, Wow, Kim Byeongkwan, and Chan. The first song they released when they first debuted was called "Cactus."

Jun and Chan auditioned for the reality series *The Unit*, and Chan was able to make it to the final group, which was called UNB. He was promoting with UNB while his other members released a repackaged album on June 7, 2018 titled *Adventures in Wonderland*.

Aegyo

Aegyo is a form of physical expression where you overemphasize displays of cuteness. There are various songs and actions that commonly show this "aegyo" amongst the Korean entertainment industry. A lot of artists are put on the spot to show their aegyo on various variety shows and programs as it is said to be a form of expression that fans enjoy seeing.

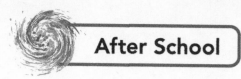

After School

After School was formed under the company Pledis Entertainment. They debuted in January 2009 with the song "AH!"

Because the concept of the group is an admission and graduation system, the members of the group have constantly been changing. The original members of After School were Soyoung, Bekah, Kahi, Jooyeon, and Jungah. Other members who were part of the group include Kaeun, Lizzy, Nana, E-Young, UEE, and Raina. The current members are Raina, Nana, E-Young, and Kaeun.

After School Club (ASC)

After School Club is a popular Internet-based music show. Jang Han-Byul and Eric Nam were the hosts of the show when it first aired in 2013, but the show has gone on to have various other hosts—some of which are K-pop idols. The show brings popular K-pop idols and groups onto the show and then connects them with fans from all over the world. It's a great platform for the fans to ask their favorite groups and group members some questions and request them to do fun things.

Aigoo

A term used to express oneself when you are frustrated or when you make a mistake. It is equivalent to saying, "oh no!" or "oops."

E.g., "Aigoo! I dropped my glass of water!"

Ailee

Ailee is a Korean American singer who was born in Denver, Colorado on May 30, 1989. She grew up in New Jersey and moved to South Korea to pursue her singing career in 2010. She signed under YMC Entertainment and released her single, "Heaven," in 2012. Ailee gained a lot of popularity, especially through her YouTube channel where she uploaded various covers of songs. When she dropped her first album, *VIVID*, in September of 2015, there was a lot of anticipation and excitement, especially considering her powerhouse vocal abilities. Her natural ability to sing so flawlessly brought her the opportunity to sing on various variety shows and be featured on various OSTs.

Akdong Musician

Akdong Musician is a K-pop duo that is signed under YG Entertainment. This brother-sister duo were participants on the second season of the reality singing show *K-Pop Star* in 2012. Lee Chan-Hyuk was recognized for his songwriting abilities and Lee Su-Hyun was noted for her natural singing ability. After they won the program, they decided to sign with YG Entertainment.

On April 7, 2014, Akdong Musician's highly anticipated album was released. The title of the album was *Play* and they released three music videos for the three songs they were promoting. The first song they promoted was titled "200%," which was chosen by the CEO of YG, Yang Hyun Suk. It won the Song of the Year Award at the Melon Music Awards as well as the Gaon Chart K-Pop Awards.

Akdong Musician released their first EP, titled *Spring*, on May 4, 2016, and then their second studio album, *Winter*, was released on January 3, 2017. Their song "Last Goodbye" won them the Digital

Bonsang at the Golden Disc Awards in 2018, as well as the Song of the Year at the Gaon Chart K-Pop Awards.

All-kill

When a K-pop song is released by an artist or group and becomes number one on all of the major music charts in South Korea at the same time.

AllKpop

AllKpop is a K-pop website that covers news pertaining to the K-pop world. It also provides a forum for fans to leave comments and engage with each other.

Amoeba Culture

Amoeba Culture is a record label that was founded in 2006 by the hip-hop duo Dynamic Duo. Their label focuses on R&B and rap artists, and is home to several popular artists, such as Primary, Crush, and Rhythm Power.

Angels

Name for the fandom of K-pop boy group Teen Top. The previous unofficial name for their fans was Andromeda; however, the group officially dubbed their fans as "Angels."

Antenna Music

Antenna Music is a record label that was founded by producer Yoo Hee-Yeol in 1997. The agency houses solo artists Sam Kim, Kwon Jin-Ah, Jung Seung-Hwan, Lee Jin-Ah, Lee Soo-Jung, and Park Sae-Byul.

Antis

In the K-pop world, people who are against a specific K-pop group or artist are called antis. These people usually like to exude their distaste and hate for certain groups and artists online by posting negative comments.

AOA

AOA, which is an acronym for "Ace of Angels," is signed under FNC Entertainment. The group debuted in 2012 and originally started with eight members: Jimin, Yuna, Hyejeong, Mina, Seolhyun, Chanmi, Choa, and Youkyung. Choa left the group in 2017 and Youkyung left the group in 2016, making AOA a six-member group.

On February 6, 2014, AOA won first place for the first time on the music program *Inkigayo* for their song "Miniskirt." The group released their first mini-album on June of 2014, promoting their title song, "Short Hair." The album ranked number one on various charts. They released their second mini-album, *Like a Cat*, on November 11, 2014, and got their second win on *Show Champion* for the title song of the same name. On January 2, 2017, AOA released their first full album in Korea, titled *Angel's Knock*.

AOA Black

AOA Black is a sub-unit group of AOA. The original members were Jimin, Yuna, Mina, Youkyung, and Choa, but Youkyung and Choa have since left the group. On July 26, 2013, their debut single album, titled *Moya*, was released.

AOA Cream

AOA Cream is a sub-unit group of AOA that was formed in 2016. The members are Yuna, Hyejeong, and Chanmi. On February 11, 2016, they debuted with the single titled "I'm Jelly Baby."

AOMG

AOMG, which stands for "Above Ordinary Music Group" or "Always On My Grind," is a record label that was founded by Jay Park. The artists under the agency include Cha Cha Malone, DJ Wegun, DJ Pumpkin, Elo, Gray, Hep, Hoody, Loco, Simon Dominic, Ugly Duck, Woo Won-Jae, Chan Sung-Jung, and Code Kunst. Simon Dominic was originally a cofounder, but stepped down in July of 2018 to focus on his music. The agency is known mainly for producing R&B and rap songs.

The artists in the agency have gone on several tours across America and South Korea and continue to rise in popularity.

Apink

Apink is a girl group signed under Plan A Entertainment (formerly known as A Cube Entertainment). The group initially had seven members, but one of the members, Hong Yoo Kyung, left the group in 2013. The remaining six members are Park Cho-Rong, Yoon Bo-Mi, Jung Eun-Ji, Son Na-Eun, Kim Nam-Joo, and Oh Ha-Young.

The group made their debut in 2011 with their title song, "I Don't Know," off their mini-album, *Seven Springs of Apink*. On January 5, 2012, they got their first music program win for their song "My My" on the music program *M Countdown*. Since then, they have released two more studio albums in Korea: *Pink Memory* in 2015 and *Pink Revolution* in 2016. Their Japanese albums were *Pink Season* (2015) and *Pink Doll* (2016).

Apink has been consistent in releasing chart-topping hits and have been recognized for their success by winning several impressive awards. They won Best New Female Artist at the Mnet Asian Music Awards in 2011, the Digital Bonsang at the Golden Disc Awards in 2014, and the Bonsang Award at the Seoul Music Awards in 2014, 2015, and 2016.

The group has also been quite active on variety shows and dramas. They've been guests on popular shows like *Running Man*, *2 Days & 1 Night*, *Ask Us Anything*, *Weekly Idol*, and *We Got Married*. A few of the members have also starred in various Korean dramas.

April

April is a girl group that is signed under DSP Media. The original members of the group were Hyunjoo, Naeun, Yena, Somin, Chaewon, and Jinsol. In August of 2015, the six members debuted with the release of their EP titled *Dreaming*. A few months later, Somin left the group.

In April of 2016, the five members released their second EP, titled *Spring*. In October that same year, Hyunjoo left the group and was replaced by two new members, Chaekyung and Rachel. In early 2017, the new group released their third EP, titled *Prelude*, and then their fourth EP, *Eternity*, in September. That same year, April won the K-Pop Artist Award at the 25th Korean Culture & Entertainment Awards.

ARMY (BTS fandom)

ARMY is the name given to the large fandom belonging to BTS. The meaning of ARMY is twofold. ARMY is an acronym for "Adorable Representative M.C. for Youth." The second meaning is the literal meaning of "army," which coincides with what BTS stands for, which is "Bulletproof Boy Scouts." BTS is a group that wants to shine light on the importance of youth and their "army" are the ones supporting them. An army can not be without their "bulletproof" armor.

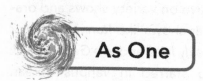

As One

As One is an R&B duo that debuted in 1999. The members are Lee Min and Crystal. The first album they released was titled *Day By Day*, which was received very well by the public. They have gone on to release five more studio albums and are currently under the agency Brand New Music.

A.S. Red & Blue

A.S. Red & Blue were special unit groups of After School. A.S. Red included members Kahi, Jungah, Uee, and Nana. A.S. Blue consisted of Jooyeon, Raina, Lizzy, and E-Young. They both released single albums that each consisted of two songs.

Asia Artist Awards

The Asia Artist Awards (AAA) is an award ceremony dedicated to television, film, and music. The AAA is fairly new, as it started in 2016. Some notable K-pop artists who have received this award are EXO (Daesang in 2016 and 2017), BTS (Best Artist Award in 2016), Seventeen (Best Artist Award in 2017), and NCT 127 and Black Pink (Rookie Award in 2016).

Asia Song Festival

The Asia Song Festival (ASF) has been held since 2004. It is a festival that brings singers and artists together from all over Asia. All artists who perform at this festival receive an award of appreciation. BoA and TVXQ were the first two artists from Korea to perform at this event in November of 2004. Some other artists who have represented South Korea include SHINee, 2PM, Girls' Generation, BIGBANG, 2NE1, Super Junior, EXO, and Red Velvet.

Ask Us Anything

Ask Us Anything, also known as *Knowing Brothers*, is a popular variety show that airs on JTBC every Saturday. The show has regular cast members Kang Ho-Dong, Seo Jang-Hoon, Kim Young-Chul, Lee Soo-Geun, Kim Hee-Chul, Min Kyung-Hoon, and Lee Sang-Min. The show started in 2015 and, although it wasn't that successful when it first came out, it has since become one of the most talked about and popular variety shows. Every week, the show features guests that answer a series of questions and partake in some funny skits and activities. These guests are usually K-pop groups, idols, actors/actresses, athletes, or comedians. They do various segments that fans enjoy seeing and are hilarious to watch.

Astro

There are six members in Astro: MJ, JinJin, Eunwoo, Moon Bin, Rocky, and Sanha. They were formed by Fantagio in 2016 and debuted with their single, "Hide & Seek."

The group starred in a web series called *To Be Continued*, alongside the actress Kim Sae-Ron and actor Seo Kang-Joon. They also had their own reality show in 2016 titled *Astro OK! Ready.*

On February 23, 2016, Astro released their first EP, titled *Spring Up.* It did considerably well on the charts as it was number four on the Gaon Music Chart. On July 1, the group released their second EP, *Summer Vibes*, which also did well. Their third EP, *Autumn Story*, was released on November 10. They have been quite busy as they released their fourth EP, Dream *Part.01* on May 29 and their fifth, *Rise Up*, on July 24, 2018.

Their group member Cha Eun Woo has been active on various variety shows as well as K-dramas. He was in the series *The Best Hit*, and starred in *ID: Gangnam Beauty.*

B.A.P

B.A.P (Best Absolute Perfect) was formed under TS Entertainment in 2012. There are six members in the group: Bang Yongguk, Youngjae, Jongup, Himchan, Daehyun, and Zelo. In 2012, they made their debut with the single "Warrior."

B.A.P released their first studio album, titled *First Sensibility*, in February of 2014. It proved to be quite successful as it topped the Gaon Monthly Chart and also the Billboard World Albums Chart. Their second album, *Noir*, was released on November 7, 2016.

B.A.P has won almost every award that they have been nominated for. Some of the more notable awards include Best Male Rookie (2012), World Rookie (2013), Hot Trend Award (2015) at the Gaon Chart K-Pop Awards, Best New Artist (2012) and Bonsang Award (2013) at the Seoul Music Awards, and the Bonsang Award (2017) at the Soribada Best K-Music Awards.

B1A4

Formed under WM Entertainment, B1A4 debuted in April of 2011 with their single, "O.K.," off their *Let's Fly* EP. The members of the group are CNU, Jinyoung, Sandeul, Baro, and Gongchan. CNU is the leader of the group and also the oldest. Jinyoung produces a lot of the music for the group.

The meaning of their group name comes from the fact that one of the members has the blood type B and the remaining four members have blood type A.

B1A4 released three studio albums in Korea and five in Japan. They won the Disc Bonsang Award at the 27th Golden Disc Awards, the Bonsang Award at the Seoul Music Awards in 2014 and 2015, and the Disc Bonsang Album Award at the 29th Golden Disc Awards.

On June 30, 2018, Jinyoung's and Baro's contracts came to an end and their agency confirmed that the two would not re-sign with the agency.

Baby

Baby is the name of the fandom for B.A.P. It means "Baby Always Behind You."

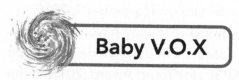

Baby V.O.X

Baby V.O.X, which means "Baby Voices of Xpression," was a first generation girl group that was formed in 1997. The original members were Lee Hee-Jin, Kim E-Z, Cha Yu-Mi, Jung Shi-Woon, and Jang Hyun-Jung. Cha Yu-Mi was replaced by Kan Mi Youn as Yu-Mi had some personal health issues to deal with. By the second album, Shi-Woon and Hyun-Jung were no longer part of the group. There were two new members added to the group, named Shim Eun-Jin and Lee Gai. It was after this change that they released their second album, titled *Baby V.O.X II*. They became well known for the title track of this album, which was "Ya Ya Ya." Lee Gai left the

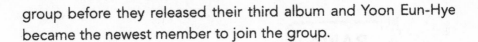

group before they released their third album and Yoon Eun-Hye became the newest member to join the group.

Baek Ji-Young

Baek Ji-Young was born on March 25, 1976. In 1999, she made her debut by releasing her first album, *Sorrow*. Her second album, *Rouge*, became a big hit and she quickly became a popular dance artist. Since *Rouge*, Baek Ji-Young has released six more albums and is known to sing a lot of popular K-drama theme songs. Some songs that she is most known for are "Like Being Hit by a Bullet," "That Woman" (*Secret Garden* OST), "Don't Forget Me" (*Iris* OST), and "After a Long Time" (*Rooftop Prince* OST).

Bagel girl/boy

The term used to describe celebrities who have baby-faces and glamorous bodies. An example of a well-known "bagel girl" is ex–After School member UEE. An example of a "bagel boy" is MONSTA X's Shownu.

Ban-mal

Ban-mal is the term used to refer to people conversing to each other in a casual and comfortable manner. In the Korean culture, there is a polite way of speaking, which is called jon-daet-mal. When two people first meet, it is a sign of respect to speak in jon-daet-mal. If people become closer and more comfortable with each other, one may request to stop using jon-daet-mal and to use ban-mal.

BANA

The name of the K-pop group B1A4's fandom. "BA" is supposed to refer to B1A4 and the "NA" is a reference to the fans. It is also said to be a short-formed version of the saying "Ban-ha-da" in Korea, which means "falling in love," in which case B1A4 is in love with their fans.

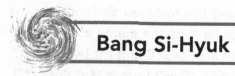

Bang Si-Hyuk

Bang Si-Hyuk was born on August 9, 1972, and is a well-known producer, songwriter, and CEO of the record company Big Hit Entertainment. He is a good friend of Park Jin-young and the two producers often made music together in the past. When Park Jin-young started JYP Entertainment, Bang Si-Hyuk would help produce a lot of his artists' songs and albums. Some artists that he has helped produce music for were g.o.d, Rain, Wonder Girls, 2AM, and Teen Top.

In 2005, Bang Si-Hyuk left JYP Entertainment and started his own agency, Big Hit Entertainment. The agency is famous for being the home to the internationally famous K-pop group BTS. Bang Si-Hyuk has also won many prestigious and well-recognized awards such as the Songwriter Award at the Melon Music Awards (2016), Best Executive Producer at the Mnet Asian Music Awards (2016), Best Producer Award at the Golden Disc Awards (2017), Producer of the Year Award at the Gaon Chart Music Awards (2017), and Producer Award at the Seoul Music Awards (2018).

Bastarz

Bastarz is a sub-unit group of the K-pop group Block B that was formed in 2015. The members are B-Bomb, U-Kwon, and P.O. Their EP album, *Conduct Zero*, was released on April 13, 2015, and the title song, *Zero for Conduct*, reached number three on the Gaon Album Chart. There were several other singles that also made it on the chart. The group released their second EP, *Welcome 2 Bastarz*, on October 31, 2016.

BBC

The term referring to Block B's fans, which is an abbreviation for "Block B Club." Their fans also go by the term "honeybees," as Block B's official fan colors are black and yellow.

Beenzino

Beenzino was born on September 12, 1987. He is a rapper who is under the label Illionaire Records. Beenzino first became known on the music scene when he first started collaborating with hip-hop producer Primary. In 2012, he released his first album, titled *24:26*.

Ben

Ben was born on July 30, 1991, and is a solo Korean ballad singer. She used to be a member of the group Bebe Mignon, but is more well-known as a solo artist. She released her first album, titled

147.5, in October of 2012. Her second EP was titled *My Name Is Ben* and it was released in August of 2015. Ben has also become known for her contribution to K-drama soundtracks, and the songs have resulted in a lot of success. Some of her popular OST songs include "You" (*Healer*), "Darling You" (*Oh My Venus*), "Misty Road" (*Love in the Moonlight*), and "Stay" (*Oh My Ghostess*).

Bestfriend

Bestfriend is the name of the fandom for the K-pop group BOYFRIEND.

Bias

The term used by K-pop fans to distinguish who their favorite member is in a group. It can also refer to solo artists and singers. You are biased towards this specific person, so they are your favorite.

E.g., "Who is your bias in BTS?"
"My bias is Jimin!"

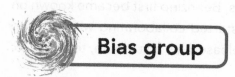

Bias group

A common term used to tell people who your most favorite K-pop group is.

E.g.,"Who is your bias group?"
"My bias group has always been BIGBANG and always will be!"

Bias list

There are many K-pop fans who have a list of biases. Meaning they have a list of K-pop idols/artists who they like enough to put on their bias list. This list can also include other popular Korean celebrities.

E.g., "G-Dragon is on my bias list. So are Onew and Taecyeon."

Bias wrecker

When a fan already has a favorite member ("ultimate bias" or "bias"), but there is another member, singer, or artist who is very close to being the most favorite.

E.g., "My bias in BTS is Jimin, but lately I've been liking Jungkook's new style. He's my bias wrecker."

The Big 3

The Big 3 consists of the three biggest K-pop agencies in South Korea: YG Entertainment, JYP Entertainment, and SM Entertainment. These labels create most of the successful K-pop groups in the industry.

Big Hit Entertainment

Big Hit Entertainment, otherwise known as BigHit, is a music label that was founded by Bang Si-Hyuk in 2005. The agency is mostly known for being the home of BTS, but it is also home to artist Lee Hyun.

BIGBANG

BIGBANG is a five-member boy group that is signed under YG Entertainment. The members of BIGBANG include G-Dragon (GD), T.O.P, Taeyang, Daesung, and Seungri. They debuted in 2006 with the album *Bigbang Vol. 1* and became popular for their single, "Lies." The song, which was produced by G-Dragon, won Song of the Year at the 2007 Mnet Asian Music Awards and Record of the Year in Digital Release at the Seoul Music Awards in 2008.

BIGBANG continued to reign on the music charts with more singles, which included "Day By Day," "Blue," "Fantastic Baby," "Loser," "Bang Bang Bang," "Bae Bae," "Loser," "Fxxx It," and "Last Dance"—to name a few!

All of the members have also embarked on solo activities, each of them releasing at least one album. G-Dragon has become a monumental figure in terms of K-pop idols who produce, and T.O.P has starred in several films and K-dramas. As of 2018, Daesung, G-Dragon, T.O.P, and Taeyang have all enlisted into the army for their mandatory service.

Birthday Ads

In South Korea, it is common for fandoms to gather money to advertise their favorite K-pop idol's birthday. These come in various forms, like banners, posters, big screens in the midst of busy neighborhoods or areas, on subway buses, or inside the stations, etc. It is a sign to show support for their favorite idols and to celebrate the day they were born!

Blackjacks

Blackjacks is the name of YG Entertainment's former girl group 2NE1's fans. The fans are referred to as "Blackjacks," as in the card game Blackjack, in which you have to get 21 to win the game.

BLACKPINK

BLACKPINK is a four-member girl group that was formed under YG Entertainment. This was the first time in six years that YG had formed a girl group since 2NE1. The members of BLACKPINK are Jisoo, Jennie, Lisa, and Rosé. BLACKPINK debuted in the summer of 2016 with the song "Whistle." Their second single was "Boombayah." These two songs were megahits, and they were even able to to win first place on the music program *Inkigayo*, just thirteen days after their debut. This was considered to be the shortest amount of time for any girl group to have gotten the number-one spot so shortly after debuting.

Their success continued with hit songs "Playing with Fire," "Stay," "As If It's Your Last," and "Ddu-Du Ddu-Du." The music video for their song "Ddu-Du Ddu-Du" gained the highest number of views for a girl group on YouTube within twenty-four hours.

Blink

Blink is the official fandom name for fans of BLACKPINK.

Block B

Block B is a seven-member K-pop boy group which consists of members Jaehyo, U-Kwon, Park Kyung, Zico, Taeil, B-Bomb, and P.O. Zico is the leader of the group and also produces a lot of the songs on their albums.

The group debuted in 2011 with a music video for their song, "Freeze." The song got some backlash as it was deemed too inappropriate to air on Korean television. The group made their live debut performance in April of 2011 on the music program KBS *Music Bank*.

Their first studio album, *Blockbuster*, was released on October 17, 2012, and was received well. The title song, "Nillili Mambo," reached the top ten on Billboard's World Albums Chart. That same year, they won the New Artist Award at the 20th Korean Culture Entertainment Awards, as well as Best Male Video at the SBS MTV Best of the Best Awards.

BoA

BoA was born on November 5, 1986. She is an artist under the SM Entertainment label and there's really nothing she can't do. She's a dancer, singer, composer, and actress.

Considered to be the Queen of K-pop, BoA started her career at a very young age in the K-pop industry. She started training in 1998 and debuted two years later when she released the album *ID; Peace B*, which was a huge success. Two years after debuting in South Korea, she debuted in Japan with the album *Listen to My Heart*. This was a monumental breakthrough as she became the first K-pop star to promote in Japan. Her multilingual skills brought her a lot of opportunities in the US as well, and she made her Hollywood movie debut in *Make Your Move 3D*.

Body Rolls

Body rolls is a specific dance move that many K-pop fans adore. It's when the artists roll their body from head to toe in a continuous motion.

BOICE

In 2010, CNBLUE officially named their fan club BOICE. It is a combination of the words "Blue" and "Voice."

Bolbbalgan4

Bolbbalgan4 is a female duo that formed in 2016 under Shofar Music. The members are Ahn Ji-Young and Woo Ji-Yoon. They are known for their appearance on *Superstar K 6*. They released their first EP on April 22, 2016, titled *Red Ickle*, followed by their first album, *Red Planet*, on August 29, 2016. Since the release of their albums, they've been climbing the charts and gaining a lot of popularity. They were even recognized by winning New Artist of the Year at the 2017 Golden Disc Awards, Best Vocal Performance—Group at the 2017 Mnet Asian Music Awards, and Indie Discovery of the Year at the 2017 Gaon Chart Music Awards.

Boy Group

Term used to refers to a K-pop group that consists only of males.

BOYFRIEND

Signed under Starship Entertainment, BOYFRIEND debuted in May of 2011. The members are Donghyun, Hyunseong, Jeongmin, Youngmin, Kwangmin, and Minwoo. They released two songs almost back-to-back, titled "Boyfriend" and "You & I."

Boys24

Boys24 is a boy group that was formed in 2016 under CJ E&M. There were twenty-four members in the group and they were all divided into four units, which were Yellow, White, Green, and Sky.

The Boyz

The Boyz is a boy group that was formed in 2017 under Cre.ker Entertainment. There are twelve members in the group: Sanyeon, Jacob, Younghoon, Hyunjae, Juyeon, Kevin, New, Q, Ju Haknyeon, Hwali, Sunwoo, and Eric.

The group debuted with their first EP, *The First*, on December 6, 2017, and had an online mini-concert in March 2018. They released their second EP, *The Start*, on April 3, 2018, and that same year they won a Global Rookie Top 5 award at the V Live Awards and Male Rookie Idol of the Year at the Korea Brand Awards.

Brand New Music

Brand New Music is a music agency that was founded by Rhymer (Kim Se-Hwan). It is an agency that specifically signs hip-hop artists. In 2009, Brand New Production became partners with Future Flow, and they became Brand New Stardom. The agency split in 2011 into Stardom Entertainment and Brand New Music. Brand New Music became the home to artists like Verbal Jint, As One, Bumkey, and Park Woo Jin.

Brave Brothers

Brave Brothers, who is also known as Kang Dong-chul, was born on June 17, 1979. He is a famous rapper, songwriter, and producer who used to be under YG Entertainment. He started his own label in 2008 called Brave Entertainment and produced songs for many popular K-pop artists and groups. Some of the popular songs he has produced include 4Minute's "What's My Name," AOA's "Short Hair," BtoB's "Beep Beep," and Sistar19's "Ma Boy."

Brave Girls

Brave Girls is a girl group that was formed by Brave Brothers in 2011. The original members of the group were Eunyoung, Seoa, Yejin, Yoojin, and Hyeran. They debuted with the single album *The Difference*, and promoted their single titled "Do You Know." Their mini-album, *Back to da Future*, was released in July of 2011, followed by their second mini-album, *Re-Issue*, in February of 2012. It was after the release of *Re-Issue* that they became more popular.

In February of 2016, there were five new members added to the group along with Yoojin and Hyeran. The new members were Eunji, Yuna, Hayun, Yujeong, and Minyoung. They released their third mini-album, *High Heels*, in June of 2016. Yoojin left the group in early 2017 and Hyeran stepped away from the spotlight to focus on her health. The five members released their fourth mini-album, *Rollin'*, in March of 2017.

Brown Eyed Girls

Brown Eyed Girls is a girl group under Mystic Entertainment. The members of the group include JeA, Miryo, Narsha, and Gain. They spent three years training until they finally released their first album, titled *Your Story*, in March of 2006. Their genre and sound was more R&B and they also released a lot of ballad songs. They've released five more albums, as well as one album in Japan. They've all also embarked on solo activities and have appeared on various variety shows throughout the years. In 2016, the group had their ten-year anniversary and celebrated by holding a concert in Los Angeles.

Brown Eyed Soul

Brown Eyed Soul is a popular R&B boy group who debuted in 2003. The members, who are Jungyup, Naul, Youngjun, and Sung Hoon, released their first album, titled *Soul Free*, on September 18 of that year. It was an instant hit. Four years later, the group released their second album, *The Wind, The Sea, The Rain*, which was also a big hit. The group did not appear on television programs often, but were still successful as a result of their catchy and emotional songs and amazing vocalists.

BtoB

Formed under Cube Entertainment in 2012, BtoB includes members Seo Eun-Kwang, Lee Min-Hyuk, Lee Chang-Sub, Im Hyun-Sik, Peniel, Jung Il-Hoon, and Yook Sung-Jae. The group is split up into vocalists and rappers. They debuted in 2012, performing two songs, "Insane" and "Imagine," on the Korean music program *M Countdown*. Their EP, *Born to Beat*, was released shortly after.

Im Hyun Sik and Il-Hoon are known to produce a lot of the music for their albums. The group gained a lot of success and recognition for their hit single, "Missing You," the title track off their second album, *Brother Act*, which was released in October of 2017. Im Hyun Sik had produced this particular song.

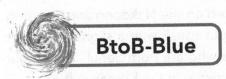

BtoB-Blue

BtoB-Blue is a sub-unit of the group BtoB. The members include BtoB vocalists Seo Eun-Kwang, Lee Chang-Sub, Im Hyun Sik, and Yook Sung-Jae. They released a digital single titled "Stand By Me" in September of 2016. Their second digital single was released on August 2, 2018, and it was titled "When the Rain Falls."

BTS

BTS, which stands for "Bangtan Sonyeondan" ("Bulletproof Boyscouts"), is a seven-member boy group that was founded under Big Hit Entertainment. Members include Jin, Suga, J-Hope, RM (Rap Monster), Jimin, V, and Jungkook. RM is the leader of the group. They debuted in June 2013 with the song "No More Dream" and released their first album, titled *2 Cool 4 Skool*. Since then, they've continued to release albums, EPs, and singles that have topped charts not only in South Korea, but also internationally.

Although they gained some popularity in Korea when they first debuted, their biggest breakthrough came when they won the Top Social Artist Award in 2017 at the Billboard Music Awards. It was an impressive feat as they were able to beat out pop superstar sensations like Justin Bieber and Selena Gomez. They were also the first-ever K-pop group to take home a Billboard Music Award trophy. They won the same award the following year in 2018.

Busan

Busan is a city located in South Korea. It is the second most populated city after Seoul and is located on the Nakdong and Suyeong Rivers. In the city of Busan, people speak with a slightly different accent, called satoori, than those who are from Seoul. The accent is quite distinct and considered unique in the Korean culture.

Many celebrities and K-pop idols make their way from Busan to Seoul in order to pursue a music career. A lot of the artists try to "fix" their satoori accent to make it sound more pleasant to hear, but it is a quality that many fans adore. Some famous K-pop stars who are from Busan include BTS's Jungkook and Jimin, CNBLUE's Jung Yong-Hwa and Lee Jong-Hyun, Wanna One's Kang Daniel and Hwang Min-Hyun, and ZE:A's Im Si-Wan.

Buzz

Buzz is a rock group that debuted in the early 2000s. Their first album, titled *Morning of Buzz*, was released in October 2003. Their success as a rock group continued until 2006 as they won the Rock Division Award at the SBS Gayo Daejeon in 2004 and the Best

Rock Performance in 2005 and 2006 at the Mnet Asian Music Awards. In 2007, the group temporarily split up as they had to enlist into the military for their mandatory service. Min Kyung-Hoon continued to promote as a solo artist and is currently a cast member on the hit variety show *Ask Us Anything*.

Call

A quick way to reply to someone when you want to say "Sure!" or "OK!"

E.g., "Let's go for coffee after work!"
"Call! Where should we go?!"

Cassiopeia

The name of fandom for TVXQ. Cassiopeia is a constellation that is made up of five stars, which is the number of members that were in the group.

CB Mass

CB Mass was a hip-hop group that debuted in 2000. The members included Choiza, Gaeko, and Curbin. Choiza and Gaeko had known each other since elementary school and, growing up with the same passion for music and hip-hop, they decided to form a hip-hop group. They debuted in 2000 with the album titled *Massmediah*, featuring popular artists Drunken Tiger and Yoon Mirae. They released their second album in 2001 and third album in February 2003; the group disbanded that same year. Choiza and Gaeko went on to form a duo later on called Dynamic Duo.

CF

CF stands for "Commercial Film." When a celebrity or artist gets to be in a CF, it is considered a very big deal as it means you are very successful and have some influence in the public. Many companies will offer lots of money for celebrities to be in their commercials.

Cha Cha Malone

Cha Cha Malone, otherwise known as Chase Vincent Malone, was born on May 25, 1987. In 2009, Malone and Jay Park started to produce music together. They released several songs online and on Jay Park's EP. In 2012, he began to work with a lot of other K-pop artists, like Girls' Generation and BoA. He continues to work with Jay under his label, AOMG.

Chang Kiha

Chang Kiha was born on February 20, 1982. He is a singer-songwriter for the indie group Kiha & the Faces. The group debuted in 2008 with the single titled "Cheap Coffee." It instantly put his group on the map as they became a popular indie rock group.

Cheongdam-dong

Cheongdam-dong is a very popular area located in the southern part of Seoul within the Gangnam district. One of the main reasons for this area's popularity is because it is where several influential entertainment buildings can be found. If you're in Cheongdam-dong, you're walking distance from SM Entertainment, JYP Entertainment, Cube Entertainment, and FNC Entertainment companies. There isn't much to see from the outside of these buildings, but on any given day, you are likely to see gushing fans standing outside the main doors in hopes of catching a glimpse of their favorite artists or groups.

Chi-maek

Chi-maek is a shortened word for chicken and beer. The "chi" is short for "chicken" in Korean, and the "maek" is short for "maek-ju," which means "beer" in Korean. It is popular to eat chicken and beer on a casual night out in social settings.

E.g., "You craving some chi-maek tonight for dinner?!"
"Call! Let's do it!"

Chocolate abs

The term used to describe someone with a defined six-pack because it looks like a chocolate bar.

Chuseok

A harvest festival that is celebrated in South Korea in the fall. It can be compared to Thanksgiving in North America.

CL

CL, also known as Lee Chae-Rin, was born on February 26, 1991. CL was first known as being the leader of the popular girl group 2NE1. She was born in Seoul, South Korea, but also spent some time growing up in Japan and France. She debuted with 2NE1 in May 2009 and sang with them until the group disbanded in 2016.

In 2014, CL signed with Scooter Braun in hopes of expanding her career into the United States. She released her first single, titled "Hello Bitches," which was followed by her EP, *Lifted*. In January 2018, CL debuted in Hollywood alongside Mark Wahlberg in the film *Mile 22*.

Clazziquai

Clazziquai is an underground electro pop group. Although their first album, *Instant Pig*, was released in 2004, they had released unofficial albums online since 2001 and had already made a name for themselves by the time their first official album was released. The members of the group are DJ Clazzi, Alex Chu, and Horan.

CLC

CLC stands for "CrystaL Clear," a K-pop girl group formed under Cube Entertainment. The group originally had five members when they released their first mini-album in March 2015, titled *First Love*. The original five were Seung-Hee, Yu-Jin, Seung-Yeon, Sorn, and Ye-Eun. Elkie and Eun-Bin joined the group in February 2016.

Cleo

Cleo was one of the original Korean idol girl groups, formed in 1999. Their members included Kim Ha-Na, Park Ye-Eun, Chae Eun-Jung, Han Hyun-Jung, and Jung Ye-Bin. Some of their hit songs included "Ready for Love," "Always in My Heart," and "Mosun."

Click-B

Click-B is a boy group that was signed under DSP Media in the late '90s. The members of the group were Woo Yun-Suk, Oh Jong-Hyuk, Kim Sang-Hyuk, Kim Tae-Hyung, Ha Hyun-Gon, Yoo Ho-Suk, and No Min-Hyuk. They released their first album in 1999, *Volume 1*. In 2003, the remaining members, Woo Yun-Suk, Oh Jong-Hyuk, Kim Sang-Hyuk, and Kim Tae-Hyung, released their fourth album. In 2011, all seven members got together again to release two new songs.

Clon

Clon consists of members Kang Won-Rae and Koo Jun-Yup. They debuted in 1996 and are known for their dance music and choreography. Their first album, *Are You Ready?*, was very well received and their success only continued to rise. Their choreographed dances, along with their catchy upbeat tunes, was what they became known for. They won Best Dance Performance at the Mnet Asian Music Awards in 2000 and were nominated for Best Male Group that same year.

CNBLUE

The "CN" in CNBLUE stands for "Code Name," and "BLUE" stands for "burning, lovely, untouchable, and emotional." The members include leader Jung Yong-Hwa on lead guitar and vocals, Lee Jong-Hyun on guitar and vocals, Kang Min-Hyuk on drums, and Lee Jung Shin on bass guitar. They are a pop-rock group that was formed in 2009 under FNC Entertainment.

CNBLUE initially made appearances and released albums in Japan, until 2010, when they successfully debuted in Korea. Their first released song, "I'm a Loner" off their *Bluetory* album, was a hit, reaching the top of the Gaon Album Chart and winning the Digital Music Bonsang Award at the 2010 Golden Disc Awards. The group has continued to be very successful as they released several more albums in Korea and also Japan, which brought them international success. They have gone on one world tour in 2013, several tours across Asia between 2010 and 2017, and more than ten tours across Japan.

All of the group members have also made their way into acting, appearing in several Korean dramas.

Co-ed

Co-ed is a term used to refer to a K-pop group that has both male and female members. Some examples of popular co-ed groups include Koyote, Akdong Musician, Cool, and K.A.R.D.

Co-Ed School

Co-Ed School was a co-ed K-pop group formed in 2010 under Core Contents Media. There were six males and four females. Their names were Soo-Mi, Tae-Woon, Sung-Min, Jung-Woo, Hyo-Young, Hye-Won, Kwang-Haeng, Kang-Ho, Chan-Mi, and Noo-Ri.

The group was split up into two sub-unit groups; all of the females became F-ve Dolls and all of the males from the group became Speed.

Co-No (Coin NRB)

Co-No is a shortened way of saying "Coin Noraebang." Coin noraebangs are very popular in Korea as people can get the karaoke experience with just a few dollars. You can usually find them in arcades or they have full stores dedicated to just the booths. "Co" is short for "coin" and "no" is short for "noraebang," which means "karaoke" in Korean.

Code Kunst

Code Kunst, whose real name is Jo Sung-Woo, was born on December 18, 1989. He is signed under HIGHGRND and is a well-known producer and rapper. He released two albums prior to signing with HIGHGRND in 2015 and released one album, titled *Muggle's Mansion*, in February 2017. Some popular songs that he has helped produce include Oh Hyuk's "Parachute" and G.Soul and Tablo's "Fire Water."

Collaboration

When an artist or group wants to feature another artist or group in their song, they refer to it as a collaboration. One example of a recent collaboration is BTS's song "Idol" featuring Nicki Minaj.

Comeback

When a K-pop group releases a new album or song after they have gone on a break, they refer to it as a "comeback."

E.g., "BIGBANG is making a comeback next month with their new album and title song."

Concept

A concept refers to the theme or general feel of a K-pop group's album. Almost every K-pop group thinks of a theme that they would generally like to convey when they release a new album or song. Their hair, clothing, photoshoots, lyrics, and feel of the album might all connect to this specific concept/theme.

Cool

Cool debuted as a co-ed group in 1994 with members Kim Sung-Soo, Lee Jae-Hoon, Yu Chae-Young, and Choi Jun-Young. By their second album, the group became a three-member group, as Yuri joined and Yu Chae-Young and Choi Jun-Young left the group. They were especially popular because their songs were very cheerful and fun to sing along to.

Cosmic Girls

Cosmic Girls is a twelve-member Korean Chinese girl group who was formed under Starship Entertainment in 2015. There were divided into four sub-unit groups by the end of the year: Wonder Unit, Joy Unit, Sweet Unit, and Natural Unit. They debuted in February 2016 with their album *Would You Like?*

Crayon Pop

Crayon Pop was formed under Chrome Entertainment as a five-member girl group. Original members included Geum-Mi, Ellin, Choa, Way, and Soyul.

The group released an EP in 2012, but it wasn't until their single, "Dancing Queen," was released that they became very popular. They were mostly known for their unique costume concepts and cute choreography. In 2017, Soyul left the group for personal reasons, and the group went down to four members.

Cross Gene

Cross Gene is a five-member boy group signed under Amuse Korea. The group consists of members of Korean, Chinese, and Japanese descent, which ties in with the meaning of their group name. Their company explains that Cross Gene is a name that takes superior genes from these different countries to form a perfect group.

Group members include Shin, Takuya, Se-Young, Sang-Min, Yong-Seok. Previous members were J.G. and Casper.

Crush

Crush, whose real name is Shin Hyo-Seob, was born on May 3, 1992. He is a popular R&B singer who is signed under Amoeba Culture. Crush debuted on April 1, 2014, when he released his single, "Sometimes." On June 5, 2014, he released his album, *Crush on You*. He got a lot of recognition when he released the song "Hug Me" featuring Gaeko and his song "Just" featuring Zion.T. In 2015, Crush was recognized for his art as he won Best R&B and Soul Album at the 12th Korean Music Awards (2015) and Best Collaboration at the 17th Mnet Asian Music Awards (2015) for his collaboration with Zion.T. on the song "Just."

Cube Entertainment

Cube Entertainment was founded in 2006 by Shing Jung-Hwa and Hong Seung-Sung, who was also the former president of JYP Entertainment. The first two groups that they launched were the girl group 4Minute and boy group Beast. Both groups gained a lot of success over the years, but 4Minute disbanded and Beast ended up leaving the company to start their own independent label. The company currently manages some big names like HyunA, BtoB, CLC, and Pentagon.

Daebak

Slang term used to refer to something or a situation as being really awesome. Can also mean to "win big."

E.g., "That BTS concert was so daebak!"

Daegu

Daegu is a city in South Korea that is located in the southeastern part of Korea. It is the fourth largest city and there are lots of things for tourists to do. The city has lots of festivals, places to shop, theaters, museums, and sports events. A lot of well-known celebrities and K-pop idols traveled from Daegu to Seoul to pursue their careers. Some well-known idols who are from Daegu include BTS's V and Suga, Red Velvet's Irene, Seventeen's S.Coups, SHINee's Key, and MONSTA X's Jooheon.

Daesang

The ultimate award given to the best artist of the year. Usually only one group or artist is given this award.

Dal Shabet

Dal Shabet includes members Ah-Young, Serri, Subin, and Woo-Hee. Previous members were Viki, Ji-Yul, and Ka-Eun. They debuted in January of 2011 with the song "Supa Dupa Diva," which was a huge success!

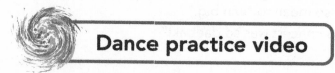

Dance practice video

One thing that K-pop fans love seeing about their favorite K-pop groups and artists is their choreography for hit songs. A lot of artists these days are releasing behind-the-scenes footage of themselves doing the complete dance for the song from beginning to end in a more casual setting and in casual clothes.

Davichi

Davichi includes members Lee Hae-Ri and Kang Min-Kyung. They are a pop duo that was formed in 2008. Davichi comes from the Korean phrase that means "shining over everything."

DAY6

DAY6 is a six-member band that was formed under JYP. The original six members were Jae, Sung-Jin, Young K, Wonpil, Do-Woon, and Jun-Hyeok. In 2016, a year after they were formed, Jun-Hyeok left the group. They released their first mini-album, called *The Day*, in 2015 with the title song "Congratulations."

Dean

Dean, whose real name is Kwon Hyuk, was born on November 10, 1992. Dean got the influence of his stage name from the famous American actor James Dean. He is a South Korean R&B singer and producer who has also released and produced music in the US. By the time Dean was eighteen years of age, he was already writing songs for K-pop artists and by the age of twenty, he was signed with the label Joombas Music Group.

In 2015, Dean made his American debut with the song "I'm Not Sorry," which featured American artist Eric Bellinger. He debuted in Korea later that same year with the song "Pour Up" featuring Zico. It didn't take long for him to get noticed, as he won the R&B Discovery of the Year Award at the Gaon Chart Music Awards in 2016 and the Best R&B and Soul Song at the Korean Music Awards that same year.

Dean released his first EP, *130 mood: TRBL*, on March 25, 2016. He won several awards for the album. Dean has continued to produce various songs and has been featured with several famous artists, including Girls' Generation's Taeyeon, Heize, Dok2, and Crush.

Debut

When a K-pop group or artist releases a song, music video, or some sort of album for the first time to the public. This debut can also come in the form of a showcase or live performance of some sort. The debut usually comes after years of strenuous training, so it is considered a big deal in the K-pop world.

Defconn

Defconn (Yoo Dae-Joon) was born on November 17, 1976. He has been a rapper since 1998, but is more known these days as being a cast member on the show *2 Days & 1 Night* and host of the show *Idol Room*.

Deux

Deux is a legendary K-pop duo from the '90s who paved the way for many K-pop artists and groups today. They were one of the first groups who incorporated hip-hop into the Korean music industry, something that people were very unfamiliar with at the time. The members Kim Sung-Jae and Lee Hyun-Do were originally back-up dancers for another Korean artist, but they decided to collaborate and form a group. They gained a lot of success with their songs and style, but they decided to split up to pursue individual careers. Tragically, shortly after Kim Sung-Jae's solo debut, he was found dead as a result of a drug overdose.

DIA

DIA, short for DIAMOND, is a girl group that is currently signed under MBK Entertainment. The current members of the group are Eunice, Jueun, Huihyeon, Jenny, Yebin, Chaeyeon, Eunchae, and Somyi. Seunghee and Eunjin were part of the group previously. The group released their first studio album on September 14, 2015, titled *Do It Amazing*. Although their album did well, their second album, *YOLO*, which was released on April 19, 2017, was even more successful.

Digital single

A single that is released by a group or artist that is only available to download online.

Dispatch Korea

Dispatch Korea is a media outlet that provides breaking news and gossip on Korean celebrities and K-pop idols.

DIVA

Originally a four-member girl group formed in the '90s by Roo'Ra member Chae Ri-Na, who was a part of the group but left in 1999. The remaining three members were Vicki, Jini, and Lee Min-Kyung. The group exuded swag and hip-hop, which is why they garnered a lot of fans and success. They disbanded in 2005.

DJ DOC

DJ DOC is a hip-hop trio that debuted in the mid '90s. The members are Lee Ha-Neul, Jung Jae-Yong, and Kim Chang-Yeol. Park Jung-Hwan was originally in the group, but left after the release of their first album. Some hit songs by DJ DOC are "Dance with DOC" and "Run to You," which still continue to be anthems in the K-pop industry.

Dok2

Dok2 (Lee Joon-Kyung) was born on March 28, 1990. He is a well-known rapper and producer in the Korean music industry. Dok2 always had a passion for rap music and even started his career at only thirteen years of age when he signed with the label Future Flow Entertainment. He was able to produce songs for artists like Drunken Tiger, Dynamic Duo, and Epik High. In 2009, Dok2 released his first mini-album, titled *Thunderground*.

In 2011, Dok2 and The Quiett formed Illionaire Records, which is a hip-hop music agency. Dok2 has been on various popular variety shows including the reality hip-hop music program *Show Me the Money* (seasons 3, 5, and 6), *Infinite Challenge*, *I Live Alone*, and *My Ugly Duckling*.

Dong-seng

The term used to call someone who is younger than you. The term can be used to refer to one's actual younger brother or sister, but it can also be used to refer to a close friend who is younger in age.

DPR Live

DPR Live (Hong Da-Bin), was born on January 1, 1993. DPR stands for "Dream Perfect Regime." On March 15, 2017, he released his first album, titled *Coming to You Live*. His second album, titled *Her*, was released on December 7, 2017.

Dream Concert

A huge concert and event that is put on every year. It features many popular K-pop groups and artists.

Dreamcatcher

Dreamcatcher, which was formerly known as MINX, is a girl group consisting of seven members. The members are JIU, SuA, Siyeon, Handong, Yoohyeon, Dami, and Gahyeon. They are signed under Happy Face Entertainment. Dreamcatcher debuted with their single album, titled *Nightmare*, on January 13, 2017.

Drunken Tiger

Drunken Tiger are considered the pioneers of Korean hip-hop. They debuted in 1999 with the album *Year of the Tiger*, with title songs "I Want You" and "Do You Know Hip-Hop?," which are still considered epic hip-hop anthems today. The frontmen of the group at the time were Tiger JK and DJ Shine, but there were other members in the group and ones who had joined later: Micki

Eyes, DJ Jhig, and Roscoe Umali. In 2013, Tiger JK started his own label, MFBTY, with his wife Yoon Mi-Rae and Bizzy. Drunken Tiger reunited in 2018 to release one final album, titled *Drunken Tiger*.

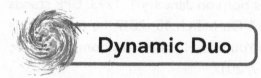

Dynamic Duo

Dynamic Duo is a hip-hop duo that was formed in 2004. The duo includes members Choiza and Gaeko who are childhood friends. They were formerly part of a group called CB Mass, but they left the group and released the album *Taxi Driver* in 2004. It became a bestselling hip-hop album as it sold more than 50,000 copies in the first month.

In 2006, the duo started their own hip-hop music agency called Amoeba Culture and shortly after, they released their third album, titled *Enlightened*.

Dynamic Duo has won Best Rap/Hip-Hop Award at the Golden Disk Awards (2017), Best Rap/Hip-Hop Award at the Melon Music Awards in 2012, 2013, and 2017, and Best Music Video (2007), Best Rap Performance (2013), and Best Collaboration (2017) at the Mnet Asian Music Awards.

E.L.F

The name for the fandom of Super Junior. E.L.F is an acronym for "Ever Lasting Friends."

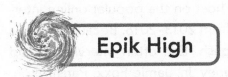

Epik High

The trio signed with Woollim Entertainment and the group made their debut in 2003 with the album titled *Map of the Human Soul*. Their second album, *High Society*, became noticeably more popular in South Korea and their third album, *Swan Songs*, was even more of a success as it reached number one on various charts. They released their fourth album, *Remapping the Human Soul*, in 2007 and it became one of the bestselling albums that year. Their fifth album was titled *Pieces, Part One* and it was released in 2008.

In 2009, Epik High left their label, Woollim Entertainment, and started their own label called Map The Soul. It consisted of artists MYK, Planet Shiver, and Dok2. After DJ Tukutz and Mithra Jin enlisted into the military, Tablo signed a contract with YG Entertainment. In October 2012, Epik High released an album under YG Entertainment and made their comeback to the music scene after taking a break for three years. The title of the album was *99*.

The success of Epik High and their impact on the mainstream hip-hop music scene in Korea is commendable. They have been awarded for their success countless times, including winning the Best Hip-Hop Artist Award at the Golden Disk Awards in 2005, 2009, 2013, and 2015.

Eric Nam

Eric Nam is a singer and songwriter who was born on November 17, 1988, in Atlanta, Georgia, and finished his studies there. After uploading a cover of himself singing on YouTube, he was invited to Korea to the show *Birth of a Great Star* 2. His appearance on this show got him a deal with B2M Entertainment as a singer.

Eric's debut was on January 2013, when he released his first EP, *Cloud 9*. He was also active as a host on the popular online international show *After School Club* from 2013–2016. Because of Eric's fluency in both Korean and English, Eric often interviewed top Hollywood stars like Robert Downey Jr., Jamie Foxx, Paris Hilton, Emma Stone, and Matt Damon. In April 2014, Eric released his single, "Ooh Ooh," and got to share a stage at the Seoul Jazz Festival with other artists like Damien Rice, Chris Botti, and Craig David. In December 2015, Eric signed with CJ E&M.

Eric Nam's success and the recognition he has received are impressive. He was dubbed "2016 Man of the Year" by *GQ Korea*, listed as one of Forbes 30 Under 30 in 2017, and even made an impression in the variety show world as he won the Best Couple Award (with MAMAMOO's Solar) at the 2016 MBC Entertainment Awards.

EvoL

EvoL is a five-member girl group under Stardom Entertainment. They debuted in 2012, but disbanded in 2015. The members of the group were Yuli, Juicy, Say, Hayanna, and J-Da.

EXID

EXID is a four-member girl group who debuted in 2012. Although they had released a single in 2012, it wasn't until 2014 that they gained popularity with their song "Up & Down." Their signature move from the song became a hit sensation. The current members of the group include Solji, LE, Hani, Hye-Lin, and Jeong-Hwa.

EXO

EXO is a South Korean Chinese K-pop boy band that was formed by SM Entertainment in 2011. When they were finally ready to make their highly anticipated debut in 2012, there were twelve members: Suho, Baekhyun, Chanyeol, D.O., Kai, Sehun, Xiumin, Lay, Kris, Luhan, Tao, and Chen. In 2014, however, and much to the dismay of their fans, Kris, Luhan, and Tao left the group, making EXO a nine-member group.

They released their first album, titled *XOXO*, in 2013, promoting their song "Growl," which became a massive breakthrough hit. They sold over a million copies and won several awards. Their second album, *EXODUS*, was released in 2015; their third album, *Ex'Act*, released in 2016; and their latest, fourth album, *The War*, was released in the summer of 2017. The success enjoyed with their first album release has carried over into these subsequent releases, all of which were bestsellers, with millions of copies being sold.

EXO-CBX

In 2016, SM Entertainment formed a sub-unit of the group EXO. Their members include Chen, Baekhyun, and Xiumin and are known as EXO-CBX (abbreviation of the first letter of their names).

They have released three EPs (Extended Plays) in total, two of which are in Korean, titled *Hey Mama!* and *Blooming Days*. The third album was released in Japanese in 2017, titled "Girls."

EXO-K

EXO-K is the sub-unit group within EXO that consists of the Korean members, who are Suho, Baekhyun, Chanyeol, D.O., Kai, and Sehun.

EXO-L

The name of EXO's fandom. The "L" in "EXO-L" refers to the word "love."

EXO-M

EXO-M is the sub-unit group within EXO that consists of the Chinese and/or Chinese-speaking members, who are Kris, Xiumin,

Luhan, Lay, Chen, and Tao. As of now, Kris, Luhan, and Tao are not members of EXO. The "M" in EXO-M stands for "Mandarin."

Eye-smile

Eye-smiles are that charming smile on a person when their eyes turn into the shape of a crescent. Some K-pop idols who are known for their eye-smiles are Apink's Jung Eun-Ji, Highlight's Lee Gi-Kwang, and former Girls' Generation member Tiffany.

Fan chant

Fans come up with chants for songs that usually match the beat and melody. The chants usually involve the names of the members and some sort of short message to cheer them on.

Fan club

Fan clubs require payments. The perks they offer are not only up-to-date news about your favorite K-pop idol or group, but they also provide priority seating at music events, early ticket access to fan meetings (and sometimes concerts), and cool merchandise.

Fan meeting

It is common for K-pop groups and artists in the Korean entertainment industry to hold fan meetings where the stars can interact with their fans. The setting is a bit more intimate and fans are able to have a chance to get more up-close and personal with their favorite celebrity.

Fan service

When an idol or celebrity gives special attention to his/her fans, they refer to it as giving "good fan service." These generous acts of fan service can include winking at specific fans, shaking each of their hands, taking extra time with them at fan meetings, and even giving them hugs. Sometimes, if fans are super lucky, the idol might show them their abs.

Fan wars

Fan wars occur when two different fandoms are at "war" with each other. Someone saying something mean about another group member can instigate a war. It can be gruelling and savage. An example of one of the most epic "fan wars" that two fandoms had with each other was back in the '90s when K-pop groups H.O.T and Sechskies were rivals. Their fans were ruthless to each other and very protective over their favorite group. Sometimes it even brought about actual physical fights.

Fanboy/Fangirl

The term used to refer to a hardcore fan of a K-pop group, artist, or K-pop in general.

fancafe

A lot of famous stars and K-pop groups/idols in Korea have an online fancafe, which fans can register to be part of. They get regular updates, photos, and access to the star's schedule, and sometimes even hear from the stars themselves!

Fancy Child

Fancy Child is a group of rappers, R&B artists, and producers who are friends and collaborate with each other musically. This group includes Zico, Penomeco, Crush, Dean, Staytuned, and Millic.

Fandom

Every K-pop group has a group of fans that they refer to as a fandom. Usually there's an official name that is given by the group or company; for example, BTS's fandom is referred to as ARMY.

Fanfiction

Fictional stories written about K-pop groups and artists. They involve love stories between group members and with other members of different groups. They take place in fictional settings with background stories about characters that can also be fictional.

FIESTAR

FIESTAR included members Linzy, Yezi, Jei, Hyemi, Cheska, and Cao. They were signed under LOEN Entertainment (now known as Kakao M) in 2012. Cheska left the group in 2014 and the rest of the group disbanded in 2018.

Flower boy

The term used to describe a male celebrity as looking very delicate and pretty. Some popular flower boys in the K-pop industry include Winner's Kim Jinwoo, SHINee's Choi Min-Ho, Infinite's L, BTS's Jin, and VIXX's Hongbin.

Fly to the Sky

An R&B duo formed in 1998 by SM Entertainment that includes members Hwanhee and Korean American Brian Joo. Their first album was released in 1999, titled *Day by Day*. Although it was their first album, the duo became instantly popular. Their second album was released in 2001, titled *The Promise*. In 2002, they released their third album, titled *Sea of Love*, and the title track for the song became an instant hit for the summer. Even more impressive is that the second track that they released, titled "Condition of My Heart," was written by American R&B singer Brian McKnight.

In 2004, Fly to the Sky left SM Entertainment and signed with PFull Entertainment. They released several more albums under this label, until 2009, when the duo decided to go their separate ways and focus on their solo albums.

In 2014, the group made a comeback and released their ninth album, titled *Continuum*. Since then, the group has continued to appear on various variety shows as well as work on their solo careers. Although Brian has taken some other career routes outside of the spotlight, Hwanhee continues to make music.

4Minute

4Minute signed under CUBE Entertainment in 2009 and released its first single, "Hot Issue," that same year. The members included leader Jihyun, Gayoon, Jiyoon, Hyuna, and Sohyun. Hyuna was previously in the group Wonder Girls and was the first member of 4Minute when the group was formed. Although the group had faced some scrutiny for their sexual content, they still managed to become very successful and popular. They won the Newcomers Award in 2009 at the 24th Golden Disc Awards and continued to win very respectable awards including the Bonsang in 2011 and 2012 at the Seoul Music Awards, Digital Bonsang in 2012 and 2014 at the Golden Disc Awards and the Bonsang at the 23rd Seoul Music Awards (2014).

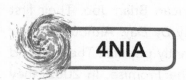

4NIA

The name of 4Minute's fandom. The name comes from a combination of their group name, 4Minute, and the word "mania."

fromis_9

fromis_9 is a girl group that came together as a result of a reality show called *Idol School*. The group members are Saerom, Hayoung,

Gyuri, Jiwon, Jisun, Seoyeon, Chaeyoung, Nagyung, and Jiheon. They are currently signed under Stone Music Entertainment. The group debuted on January 8, 2018, with the release of their EP titled *To. Heart*.

F.T. Island

The "F.T." stands for "Five Treasure." The group members include leader Choi Jong-Hoon, bass player Lee Jae-Jin, guitarist Song Seung-Hyun, drummer Choi Min-Hwan, and main vocalist Lee Hong-Ki. They are a rock band that was formed under FNC Entertainment in 2007 and released the song "Love Sick" that was a big success. F.T. Island gained a lot of international success, particularly in Japan. Before the release of their first album, they released several singles that were all successful in Japan. At one point, they even had three singles in the top ten on the Oricon charts.

F.T. Triple

F.T. Triple is a sub-unit group of F.T. Island that includes members Choi Jong-Hoon, Choi Min-Hwan, and Lee Jae-Jin. They were formed in 2009 and their first single was titled "Love Letter."

Full album

In the K-pop world, artists and groups release mini-albums or EPs that do not have a lot of songs. When they do release a full album, it usually contains about a dozen songs.

f(x)

f(x) was formed in 2009 under SM Entertainment. The group members were Victoria, Amber, Luna, Krystal, and Sulli, but Sulli left the group in 2015. They released their first single, "LA chA TA," in September 2009. In May 2010, the group released their first EP, titled *Nu ABO*, which reached number one on the charts. Their first studio album was released on April 2011, titled *Pinocchio*. In 2013, f(x)'s success was able to bring them the opportunity to do a collaboration with Anna Kendrick in the US for the show *Funny or Die*. Their second album, *Pink Tape*, reached the Billboard's K-pop Hot 100 and World Album Charts.

Gae-gasu

"Gae-gasu" is the shortened term that people use to refer to a comedian who is also a singer. "Gae" is a shortened word for "Gae-geu-man," which means "comedian" in Korean. The "gasu" part of the word means "singer" in Korean. Some popular "gae-gasu's" include Shin Bora, Haha, Park Myung-Soo, and Yoon Se-Yoon.

Gangnam

Gangnam in Korean means "south of the river." It is an area in Seoul that is known to have expensive real estate, and a lot of wealthy people reside in the district. It's an area that has lots of shopping, nice restaurants, cafes, and schools. A lot of stars and K-pop idols are known to hang out in this area and/or shop here.

Gangnam Style

"Gangnam Style" is the hit song produced by PSY. The Gangnam area in Seoul became internationally known because of this song. It was released in July 2012 and it became the first video on YouTube to reach a billion views.

Gaon Album Chart

Gaon Album Chart was launched in February of 2011. It is a music chart that ranks bestselling albums, mini-albums, and single albums.

Gaon Chart Music Awards

Gaon Chart Music Awards is a ceremony that awards K-pop artists and groups based on their albums and songs. The data is compiled based on online music platforms and collects statistics on the sales of songs and albums.

Gaon Digital Chart

Gaon Digital Chart garners all the best singles of the week, month, and year in the Korean music industry.

Gaon Music Chart

The Gaon Music Chart shows the popular songs and albums of the week. It is run by the Korea Music Content Association.

GD X Taeyang

GD X Taeyang is a sub-unit group from BIGBANG. The members of this duo are G-Dragon and Taeyang. The two were best friends since they were trainees in YG Entertainment and were even supposed to officially debut as a duo. However, three other members were added, which was how BIGBANG was formed. G-Dragon is the rapper in this unit, while Taeyang takes care of the vocals. They released their first single in 2014, titled "Good Boy," which became a big hit.

G-Dragon

G-Dragon is the leader of BIGBANG. His real name is Kwon Ji-Yong and he was born on August 18, 1988. He's known for his rap-ping skills, producing skills, fashion style, and overall swag. He trained under YG Entertainment since he was six years old until he debuted in 2006 with BIGBANG. While he was in BIGBANG, he also released solo albums, all of which were big hits.

GFriend

GFriend is a girl group that includes members Sowon, Yerin, Eunha, Yuju, SinB, and Umji. They signed under Source Music in 2015 and debuted with their EP, *Season of Glass*, early that year. They gained momentum very quickly and became successful from the release of their EP. They won Best New Artist (Female) at the Melon Music Awards the year they debuted and have continued to win awards since. They even garnered international success and popularity when they were nominated at the 2015 MTV Europe Music Awards for Best Korean Act alongside B1A4, BTS, GOT7, and VIXX.

On July 11, 2016, GFriend released their first album, titled *LOL*. The title track they promoted for the album was called "Navillera" and they were able to snag their first music show win for the single.

In 2018, GFriend had their first solo concert and also went on their first concert tour in Asia. They also signed with King Records and debuted in Japan in May.

(G)I-DLE

(G)I-DLE is a girl group that was formed in 2018 under Cube Entertainment. The members of the group are Miyeon, Minnie, Soojin, Soyeon, Yuqi, and Shuhua. They debuted with the release of their mini-album, *I Am*, in May 2018. The group also won Female Rookie Idol of the Year at the Korea Brand Awards in that same year.

Giriboy

Giriboy, whose real name is Hong Si-Young, was born on January 24, 1991. He is a rapper and producer that has been signed with the label Just Music since 2011. Giriboy became well known when he competed on the third season of the rap competition show *Show Me the Money*.

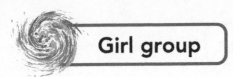

Girl group

The term used to refer to a K-pop group that consists of only females.

Girl's Day

Formed by Dream T Entertainment, Girl's Day originally had five members: Jihae, Jisun, Jiin, Sojin, and Minah. They debuted in 2010 with "Tilt My Head," and released their EP, *Girl's Day Part #1*, a couple days later.

To the dismay of their fans, just two months after the group debuted, Jisun and Jiin decided to part ways with Girl's Day and Yura and Hyeri were added. Shortly after, the newly formed group released the song "Nothing Lasts Forever." Girl's Day rose quickly in popularity when their third EP, *Everyday 2*, was released in April 2012. That same year, the group won Discovery of the Year at the Gaon Chart Music Awards. Despite their rising success, Jihae decided to leave the group before the release of their new album on October 26.

In 2013, Girl's Day became ambassadors for the organization Because I Am a Girl. Because I Am A Girl is a nonprofit organization that advocates for women's rights all around the world. They also visited Thailand to do volunteer work and did a follow-up volunteer trip a year later. In February 2016, Sojin and Yura went to Cambodia to volunteer, where they held workshops at a school. The success of Girl's Day continued to grow as they were able to snag the Global Popularity Award in 2016 at the Gaon Chart Music Awards, Digital Bonsang at the 2015 Golden Disc Awards, and the Bonsang at the 2015 Seoul Music Awards.

Girls' Generation

Girls' Generation, also known as SNSD, is a famous girl group formed under SM Entertainment. The group originally had nine members: Taeyeon, Sunny, Tiffany, Hyoyeon, Yuri, Sooyoung, Yoona, Seohyun, and Jessica. They debuted in 2007 and gained a lot of attention, but it wasn't until their hit single, "Gee," was released in 2009 that they topped the charts. It was the bestselling single that year.

In 2010, Girls' Generation debuted in Japan with the single "Genie," and shortly after released "Gee," which made it to number two on the Oricon Singles Chart. This was a huge feat considering the group was foreign to Japan. They embarked on their first tour in Japan on May 31, 2011. They were promoting their debut Japanese album, which became a huge success.

In October 2011, Girls' Generation released their third album, titled *The Boys*. To promote their album, the group made their US television debut, appearing on *The Late Show with David Letterman* and *Live with Ryan and Kelly*.

On September 29, 2014, Jessica left the group, and in 2017, Tiffany, Seohyun, and Sooyoung left SM Entertainment and signed with different agencies, but the group remains intact. Girls' Generation is considered to be one of the most successful and bestselling girl group artists of all time. They have been dubbed "The Nation's Girl Group," which represents their impact and significance on K-pop in South Korea.

G.Na

G.Na, whose real name is Gina Jane Choi, was born on September 13, 1987 in Edmonton, Alberta, Canada. She was originally supposed to be part of a girl group, but they ended up disbanding before their debut. G.Na decided to sign with Cube Entertainment where she released a duet with Rain. She followed up with the release of several EPs and one studio album, titled *Black & White*, under Cube Entertainment before leaving the agency in 2016.

g.o.d

g.o.d, which stands for "Groove Over Dose," is a five-member K-pop group that debuted in 1999. The members of the group include Park Joon-Hyung, Yoon Kye-Sang, Danny Ahn, Son Ho-Young, and Kim Tae-Woo. They debuted with the single "To Mother" off of their *Chapter 1* album and rose to fame very quickly. The song was recognized for its touching lyrics about a poor mother who spends hard-earned money on a bowl of noodles for her son. Despite the group's popularity, Yoon Kye-Sang left in 2004, but they reunited again in 2014, releasing their album *Chapter 8*.

Golden Child

Golden Child (GNCD) is a boy group that debuted in August of 2017 under Woollim Entertainment. There were originally eleven members in the group, who were Daeyeol, Y, Jangjun, Tag, Seungmin, Jaehyun, Jibeom, Donghyun, Joochan, Bomin, and Jaeseok, but Jaeseok left the group early in 2018.

Their first mini-album, *Gol-cha!*, was released on August 28, 2017, and their first music program appearance was on September 1 on *Music Bank*, where they performed the songs "DamDaDi" and "I Love You So" off their album.

On January 29, 2018, after Jaeseok's departure, the group released their second EP, titled *Miracle*. The same year, they won a V Live Award for Global Rookie Top 5.

Golden Disc Awards

Golden Disc Awards is a ceremony that honors the outstanding achievements of artists and idols in the K-pop music industry. The first ceremony was held in 1986 and was originally called the Korea Visual and Records Grand Prize Award. The name changed to Golden Disc Awards in 2011. The ceremony awards those artists whose music was released in the previous full year.

The biggest awards to be awarded during this ceremony are the Album Daesang Award and the Digital Song Daesang Award. There is also the Bonsang Award and the Digital Song Bonsang Award that are considered significant. In 2018, BTS was awarded the Album Daesang Award for their album *Love Yourself: Her* and EXO was awarded the previous four years in a row for their albums *Ex'Act*, *Exodus*, *Overdose*, and *XOXO*.

Goodbye stage

After a K-pop group or artist has completed promoting their album, they have one final performance on the music program where they get to say goodbye to their fans until they release their next single or album. They call this performance the "goodbye stage."

GOT7

GOT7 debuted in 2014 with the EP *Got It?* under JYP Entertainment. There are seven members in the group: JB, Mark, Jackson, Jinyoung, Youngjae, BamBam, and Yugyeom. They are known for their flashy dance moves that incorporate martial arts and b-boying. They have members from different parts of Asia, so the group has gained a lot of success internationally. They received the New Artist Award at the 29th Golden Disc Awards and the New Arts Award at the Seoul Music Awards in 2015. That same year, they starred in their first web drama, titled *Dream Knight*.

Since then, the group has had two world tours: Fly Tour in 2016, where they performed in cities like Tokyo, Bangkok, Dallas, Chicago, New York, Los Angeles, and Hong Kong. Their second world tour was called Eyes On You, which took place in May and June of 2018.

The group's success has also won them several prestigious awards such as the World Hallyu Star Award at the 2018 Gaon Music Chart Awards, and the Disc Bonsang Award at the 2018 Golden Disc Awards for their album *Flight Log: Arrival*.

Gray

Gray, whose real name is Lee Seong-Hwa, was born on December 8, 1986. He is a singer, rapper, and producer who is signed under AOMG. He has had an impressive streak of hit music since he debuted in 2012. On top of the AOMG artists he has worked with (Loco, Jay Park, Simon D, to name a few), he has also worked with some of the most respected Korean rappers and artists in the industry. He has produced music for Crush, Swings, Zion.T, Dok2, Shinhwa, Sik-K, Jessi, and BewhY. In 2016, Gray's success as a hip-hop producer earned him a spot as a judge on the hit reality rap series *Show Me the Money* 5.

Groovy Room

Groovy Room is a producing duo consisting of members Park Gyu-Jung and Lee Hwi-Min who are signed under H1GHR Music. Their first EP, titled *Everywhere*, was released on July 24, 2017. Although they are not very popular, they have produced several songs that many people will recognize, especially considering who they have worked with. Their repertoire consists mainly of hip-hop music, and some of the artists they have worked with include Younha, Crush, Dok2, Minzy, Hyolyn, Gaeko, Mad Clown, and Gary.

G.Soul

G.Soul, whose real name is Kim Ji-Hyun, was born on June 16, 1988. He is an R&B singer who was signed under JYP Entertainment. He was a trainee in JYP for fifteen years before he debuted on January 19, 2015 with his first EP, titled *Coming Home*. His second EP, *Dirty*, was released on September 10, 2015.

On June 6, 2017, G.Soul left JYP Entertainment and signed with the hip-hop label H1GHR Music, where he released his third EP, *Circles*. He enlisted into the military to fulfill his mandatory service on December 26, 2017, but the day before, he released his single album, *I'll Be There*, which he had written two years prior.

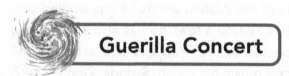

Guerilla Concert

Guerilla concert is the term used for when a K-pop group or artist has a random, unplanned performance.

Gugudan

Gugudan is a nine-member girl group that includes members Mimi, Hana, Soyee, Mina, Haebin, Nayoung, Sejeong, Sally, and Hyeyeon. They were signed under Jellyfish Entertainment and debuted in 2016 with the mini-album *Act. 1 The Little Mermaid.* Nayoung, Sejeong, and Mina were initially introduced on the show *Produce 101.* Sejeong and Mina made it to the final ten.

Gummy

Gummy is a solo artist whose real name is Park Ji-Yeon. She was born on April 8, 1981. Gummy became an instant success after she debuted in 2003 with her album titled *Like Them.* She won the Bonsang at the Golden Disc Awards in 2004 and also the Mobile Popularity Award at the Mnet Asian Music Awards that same year.

She had previously been signed with YG Entertainment, but left the agency in 2013 to sign with C-JeS Entertainment. Gummy is better known these days for her OST songs, as they usually top the charts. Gummy announced her engagement to Jo Jung-Suk in 2018.

Gwangju

Gwangju is the sixth largest city in South Korea. It is a city that is rich in culture as they have art centers, museums, theaters, and art festivals. Gwangju is also home of the KIA Tigers, which is a team that plays for the Korean Professional Baseball League. Gwangju World Cup Stadium is also known for being one of the venues used for the 2002 FIFA World Cup. Gwangju is home to many K-pop idols, including BIGBANG's Seungri, BTS's J-Hope, TVXQ's Yunho, and Suzy Bae.

H

rebuted in 2019 with the mini album 'Ace.' The Little Mermaid
Nayoung Solo: and Lane were initially introduced on the show
Produce 101 Singing are as "center maknae" to the final tes:...

Haeng-syo

This term was made popular by K-pop idol G-Dragon. It's a short-ened version of the Korean phrase "to be happy." "Haeng" is taken from the word, "Haeng-bok," which means "happiness" in Korean and the "syo" is what you would add to the end of the sentence when saying, "please."

E.g., "It was nice meeting you and catching up! Let's do it again soon sometime!"

"Absolutely! Haeng-syo until then!"

Haha

Haha, whose real name is Ha Dong-Hoon, was born on August 20, 1979. Haha originally debuted in 2001 with the group Z-Kiri, but they quickly disbanded. Haha then began to appear on variety shows including *What's Up YO!*, *Nonstop*, *X-Man*, and *Infinite Challenge*. He is better known these days as a cast member on the hit show *Running Man*.

In 2012, Haha collaborated on a mini-album with Skull, who was also a Korean reggae artist. The name of the EP was *Skull & Haha Ya Man*. In 2013, the duo made another EP, titled *REGGAErilla*.

Hallyu

The term used to describe the increasing popularity of Korean celebrities and popular culture around the world. Also referred to as the "Hallyu wave."

HALO

HALO, which stands for "Hexagon of Absolute Light and Organization," is a boy group consisting of members Dino, Ooon, Jaeyong, Heecheon, Yoondong, and Inhaeng. They debuted on June 26, 2014, with the single album titled *38°C*.

Hanbok

A traditional Korean dress that was worn in the Joseon period in history. It is usually worn for special occasions and celebrations. Many K-pop artists and celebrities wear these hanboks on special occasions and upload photos or videos of themselves on their social media accounts.

Happy Together

Happy Together is a variety talk show that airs on KBS. The show has been on air since 2001, with hosts engaging in interviews with the guests. There are many famous K-pop stars as well as celebrities who appear on the show to talk about their careers and personal lives. As of 2018, the current hosts on the show are Yoo Jae-Suk, Park Myeong-Su, Jun Hyun-Moo, Jo Se-Ho, and Uhm Hyun-Kyung.

Heize

Heize, whose real name is Jang Da-Hye, was born on August 9, 1991. She is a singer, rapper, and songwriter. Heize signed under Stone Music Entertainment and made her debut in 2014. She released a self-titled EP, *Heize*.

Heize gained a lot of popularity after releasing her single, "Star," in December of 2016, when she achieved an all-kill, topping all the music charts. In 2017, Heize released her third EP, titled *You, Clouds, Rain*, where two of her singles, "Don't Know You" and "You, Clouds, Rain," achieved all-kill status. Heize's success was also evident in all the awards she was nominated for and won. Some of the impressive awards she snagged have been the Best Vocal Performance—Female Solo at the 19th Mnet Asian Music Awards and the Digital Bonsang at the 32nd Golden Disc Awards.

Hello Venus

Joined under Pledis Entertainment and Fantagio, Hello Venus debuted with members Alice, Nara, Lime, Yooara, Yoonjo, and

Yooyoung. They debuted in 2012 with the song "Venus." In 2014, Pledis and Fantagio ended their partnership; Yooara and Yoonjo stayed with Pledis and the other four members continued with Fantagio. Fantagio added Seoyeong and Yeoreum to the group.

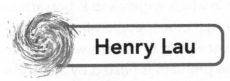

Henry Lau

Henry Lau, who was previously part of the group Super Junior-M, was born on October 11, 1989. Henry grew up in Toronto, Canada, and lived there until he passed the 2006 S.M. Entertainment Global Audition that was taking place in Toronto. In 2008, Henry debuted in the group Super Junior-M. He became well-known for his musical talents, especially on the piano and violin.

On June 7, 2013, Henry made his solo debut, releasing his EP, *Trap*. After appearing on the show *Real Men* in February of 2014, Henry became even more popular. This started his career in the variety show business as he also appeared on *Star King*, *Roommate*, *We Got Married*, and *I Live Alone*.

In April of 2018, Henry's contract with SM Entertainment came to an end. He decided to leave the agency and started his own agency called Henry's Workshop.

Hi-Touch

The "hi-touch" is a specific event that can take place at your favorite K-pop artist's and group's fan meetings. The group or artist stands in a line on one side while their fans pass by and give them a "high-five" or sometimes shake their hands. It's a very brief but meaningful opportunity for fans to yell out their "I love yous" and to make eye contact with their favorite idols!

Hidden Singer

Hidden Singer is a popular variety music show that first aired in 2013. It is a game show program in which singers and K-pop artists appear on the show to compete with other people who have similar singing voices. It is the audience's job to discern which of the voices belongs to the singer. The program is hosted by Jun Hyun Moo and five seasons have aired thus far. Some famous artists who have been on the show include Baek Ji Young, Kim Jong Kook, IU, Girls' Generation's Taeyeon, and BoA.

High4

High4 is a boy band who is signed under N.A.P. Entertainment. The original members of the group are Alex, Myunghan, Youngjun, and Sunggu; however, Sunggu departed from the group in January of 2017. They debuted in April of 2014 with the song "Not Spring, Love, or Cherry Blossoms," which also featured IU.

Highlight

Formerly known as Beast (Boys to Search for Top), Highlight is a boy band which includes members Yoon Doo-Joon, Yong Jun-Hyung, Yang Yo-Seob, Lee Gi-Kwang, and Son Dong-Woon. Jang Hyun-Seung was originally part of the group, but he departed in 2016. The group debuted in 2009 under Cube Entertainment. Their first single was called "Bad Girl," and they released a mini-album called *Beast Is the B2ST*.

In December of 2016, Beast announced that they were going to leave Cube Entertainment to start their own company called

Around Us Entertainment. The group was unable to keep their name Beast, which is why they officially changed it to Highlight.

H1GHR Music Records

H1GHR Music Records is a global record label company that was established by Jay Park and Cha Cha Malone in 2017. The label seeks to include both Korean and American hip-hop artists. The label is currently home to Sik-K, PH-1, Groovy Room, Woogie, and others.

Holland

Holland, born on March 4, 1996, debuted in January of 2018 with his single, *Neverland*. He is the first openly gay K-pop idol to debut in the industry.

Hong Jin-Young

Hong Jin-Young was born on August 9, 1985. She is a singer who debuted in 2007 with the girl group SWAN, but then her agency decided that she would be better as a trot singer, marking her solo debut in 2009. She released her single, "Love Battery," in 2009, which she won an award for at the 2009 Mnet Asian Music Awards. Aside from being a successful trot singer, Hong Jin-Young also appears on lots of variety shows, including *Immortal Songs 2*, *We Got Married*, and *Sister's Slam Dunk*.

Hongdae

Hongdae is an area located in Seoul that is known for its music scene. A lot of underground artists perform in various venues around Hongdae. It's an area that is rich in culture and surrounded by young adults, which makes for a very exciting scene.

Honorifics

In the Korean culture, there is a polite way to speak to people and a casual way to speak to people. When first meeting someone, it is customary to use "honorifics," which is a polite way of speaking. In Korean, this is called "jon-daet-mal."

Hoobae

Hoobae is the term used by sunbaes. It is a way of referring to someone who has been working in the same K-pop field for a shorter period of time.

E.g., "He started working at this company a year after me. He's my hoobae."

Hoody

Hoody, whose real name is Kim Hyun-Jung, was born on February 10, 1990. She is a singer-songwriter who signed with AOMG in 2015. Her EP titled *On and On* was released on December 16, 2016.

Hoon-nam/Hoon-nyeo

The term used to refer to someone who is charming and gives off a very warm aura. Hoon-nam is if the person is male and hoon-nyeo is if the person is female.

E.g., "Kang Daniel from Wanna One is such a hoon-nam!"

H.O.T

H.O.T is an acronym for "High-Five of Teenagers." They are the original K-pop boy group that debuted in 1996 under SM Entertainment. The members included leader Moon Hee-Joon, Jang Woo-Hyuk, Tony An, Kangta, and Lee Jae-Won. Their first single was "Descendants of Warriors" off of their *We Hate All Kinds of Violence* album, but it wasn't until their second single, "Candy," that their popularity rose. Many K-pop groups continue to do dance covers of this song today.

Since then, they released four more albums that were all huge hits. They gained a lot of fame internationally as well and were one of the first K-pop groups to start the Hallyu wave. The group disbanded in 2001, but were able to reunite through the program *Infinite Challenge* in February of 2018.

HOTSHOT

A six-member boy group which includes members Junhyuk, Timoteo, Noh Tae-Hyun, Ha Sung-Woon, Yoonsan, and Hojung. They debuted in October of 2014 with their album *Take a Shot*. Noh Tae-Hyun and Ha Sung-Woon were contestants in the second season of *Produce 101*. Noh Tae-Hyun got eliminated, but Ha Sung Woon became a part of the show's group, Wanna One.

Huh Gak

Huh Gak was born on January 5, 1985. He is a singer who won the second season of the reality singing show *Superstar K*. He signed under Plan A Entertainment and debuted with the single "Always." In November of 2010, he released his mini-album titled *Huh Gak 1st Mini Album*. Huh Gak has continued to release EPs and has partaken in singing for *Man to Man* OSTs, which has won him several notable awards, some of which include Best New Artist at the 3rd Melon Music Awards, Best New Male Artist at the 13th Mnet Asian Music Awards, Best Solo Artist at the 2011 Bugs Music Awards, and the Bonsang at the 22nd Seoul Music Awards.

Hul

The expression used when one is flabbergasted or surprised by a specific situation. It can also be used to express a feeling of frustration.

E.g., "Hey, did you hear that tickets for GOT7 sold out in 3 minutes?"

"Hul . . . why do all these K-pop tickets always sell out so fast?!"

Hwaiting/Fighting

A term used to encourage and show support. It is used in the same way the phrase, "good luck" would be used. In the Korean language, there is no letter for the sound "F," which is why they use the sound "H" as it is the closest sounding letter in terms of pronunciation.

E.g., "I'm worried about this test." "You'll do great, hwaiting!"

Hwang Chi-Yul

Hwang Chi-Yul was born on December 3, 1982. Although he debuted in 2007 and released two albums, his company shut down, leading him to take on various part-time jobs. He even got a job as a vocal coach and worked with many idol groups like Infinite, Loveleyz, and NU'EST.

In 2015, Hwang Chi-Yul's life completely changed when he appeared on the music reality show *I Can See Your Voice*. People were blown away by his voice and talent. He released a mini-album in 2015 titled *Be Ordinary* and continued to appear on various variety shows. He has also garnered a huge fan base in China.

Hyuk Shin

Hyuk Shin was born on June 5, 1985. He is a well-known producer in the K-pop world. Some popular artists he has produced songs for include EXO, Teen Top, Girls' Generation, SHINee, VIXX, f(x), TVXQ, Super Junior, Dean, MONSTA X, and AOA.

Hyukoh

Hyukoh is an indie band that was formed in 2014. The members of the group include Oh Hyuk, Im Dong-Geon, Lim Hyun-Jae, and Lee In-Woo. In September of 2014, the group released their first EP, titled *20*. The following year, the group appeared on the popular variety show *Infinite Challenge*, where they became more noticeable to the public. They released their second EP, *22*, on May 28, 2015, which was received very well. On July 21, 2015, Hyukoh signed with HIGHGRND.

Hyung

The term used by a male to refer to another male who is older than him. It is a term of endearment and is also a term used to refer to one's actual older brother.

I

I Live Alone

I Live Alone is an MBC variety show that follows the lives of celebrities and K-pop stars who live by themselves. It provides an up-close and personal look into how certain famous people live their day-to-day lives. Some famous K-pop idols who have been featured on the show include CNBLUE's Kang Min-Hyuk, Highlight's Yang Yo-Seob and Lee Gi-Kwang, f(x)'s Amber, Henry Lau, BIGBANG's Taeyang and Seungri, and TVXQ.

I.B.I

I.B.I is a girl group that was formed in 2016 under LOEN Entertainment. The members of the group are Lee Hae-In, Kim So-Hee, Yoon Chae-Kyung, Lee Su-Hyun, and Han Hye-Ri. Although they are all from different agencies, LOEN Entertainment formed them as the contestants who were runner-ups on the popular K-pop idol reality series *Produce 101*.

In August of 2016, the group released their first digital single album, titled *Molae Molae*, and appeared on the music program *M Countdown*.

Idol

The term used to describe a guy or girl who is in a K-pop group or is a K-pop artist. Once someone gets into a company and starts training to become an "idol" they are considered to be an idol even if they have not debuted yet. Their level of popularity does not matter.

Idol Room

Idol Room is a variety show that airs on JTBC. It is hosted by Jeong Hyeong-Don and Defconn. The show invites K-pop idols and groups as guests where they engage in fun games and have funny interviews. The first episode aired on May 12, 2018.

Idol Star Athletic Championships

Idol Star Athletic Championships is an event that is broadcast on MBC. It is a sports event that incorporates various K-pop idols to compete against each other. Some of the sports that the idols compete in are hurdles, relays, long jump, high jump, javelin, archery, swimming, table tennis, and gymnastics.

iGOT7

iGOT7 is the official name for GOT7's fandom. They are also referred to as "ahgase."

iKon

iKon is a seven-member K-pop group signed under YG Entertainment. The leader of the group is B.I and the other members are Jinhwan, Yunhyeong, Bobby, Donghyuk, Ju-Ne, and Chanwoo. They released their debut album in 2015 titled *Welcome Back*. Their second album was released in 2018 and was called *Return*.

iKONIC

The name of the fandom for the group, iKon.

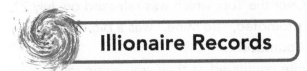

Illionaire Records

Illionaire Records is a record label that was formed by The Quiett and Dok2. What makes this label unique is that they only have one artist, Beenzino, signed to their agency. Dok2 and The Quiett have made several appearances as producers and judges on the popular hip-hop reality series *Show Me the Money*.

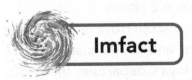

Imfact

A K-pop boy group signed under Star Empire Entertainment. The members include Jeup, Taeho, Jian, Sang, and Ungjae. They debuted in 2016 with the song "Lollipop."

IN2IT

IN2IT is a boy group that was debuted in October of 2017. The members are Jiahn, Yeontae, Inho, Hyunuk, Isaac, Inpyo, and Sunghyun. Jinsub was formerly part of the group, but he left in 2018.

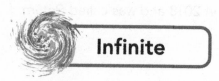

Infinite

Infinite was signed by Woollim Entertainment with members Sungkyu, Dongwoo, Woohyun, Sungyeol, L, Sungjong, and Hoya. They debuted in 2010 with the mini-album, *First Invasion* and promoted the songs "Come Back Again" and "She's Back." Their first full album was titled *Over the Top*, which was released on July 21, 2011. The single they promoted, "Be Mine," was a big hit and they won first place on *M Countdown*.

The success of Infinite continued as they won some impressive awards, including the Disc Bonsang Award and Hallyu Icon Award at the 2012 Golden Disc Awards, Best Male Group at the 2013 Mnet Asian Music Awards, and the Disc Bonsang Award at the Golden Disc Awards in 2013, 2014, 2015, and 2017.

On September 11, 2014, the group became the first K-pop group to top the Billboard Twitter Emerging Artist for their song "Last Romeo," which was off their *Season 2* album.

On June 28, 2017, all of the members except Hoya renewed their contracts with Woollim Entertainment and on August 30, 2017, Hoya officially left the group. After Hoya's departure, the group released their third album, *Top Seed*.

Infinite F

A sub-unit group from Infinite, including members Sungyeol, L, and Sungjong. They released single albums called *Koi no Sign* and *Azure*.

Infinite H

Another sub-unit group from Infinite, which included members Dongwoo and Hoya. They released their album, *Fly High*, in 2013.

Inkigayo

Inkigayo is an SBS music program that airs every Sunday. It showcases various K-pop groups and artists, providing them with a chance to promote their new songs. At the end of each show, there are three top groups or artists who are announced, which is determined by combining how well their singles/albums do on various charts. The viewers then get to vote amongst the three, which determines the number-one winner of the week.

Inspirit

The name that refers to the K-pop group Infinite's fandom.

I.O.I

I.O.I (acronym for Ideal of Idol) is an eleven-member girl group that was made as a result of a reality show called *Produce 101* in 2016. The members of I.O.I are Lim Na-Young, Kim Chung-Ha, Kim Se-Jeong, Jung Chae-Yeon, Zhou Jieqiong, Kim So-Hye, Yoo Yeon-Jung, Choi Yoo-Jung, Kang Mi-Na, Kim Do-Yeon, and Jeon So-Mi. They debuted with their EP, *Chrysalis*, in May of 2016 and disbanded in 2017, as all the members returned back to their agencies.

It's Dangerous Beyond the Blankets

It's Dangerous Beyond the Blankets is a show that highlights various K-pop idols and celebrities who are considered homebodies. The guests are put in a home and are forced to interact each other. They create friendships and bonds while staying in the house together as they all share the common trait of being more introverted and preferring to stay at home over going out. The show's pilot season aired from August to October of 2017, and a second season aired from April to July of 2018. Some popular K-pop idols who have been on the show include Highlight's Yong Jun-Hyung, EXO's Xiumin, Winner's Song Min-Ho, Wanna One's Kang Daniel, NCT's Mark, and iKon's Koo Jun-Hoe.

Itaewon

Itaewon is an area in Seoul, South Korea. It is popular for its multiculturalism as a lot of foreigners reside in the area. It is also known for its nightlife, considering all the eclectic bars, cafes, and restaurants that are located there. You can find food of various cultures in the area and it is a popular place for tourists to venture to. Several celebrities have set up restaurants and cafes in the area, which is mentioned in the songs sung by various artists.

IU

IU, whose real name is Lee Ji-Eun, was born on May 16, 1993. She is a popular singer, songwriter, and actress. IU joined LOEN Entertainment in 2007 where she began training to become a K-pop star. After almost a year of training, IU made her debut with the release of her single, "Lost Child," which was off her EP, *Lost and Found*. Although her album was not well-received, she continued to strive for success by releasing more singles and albums. By 2009, IU's appearances on various variety shows brought her more popularity. In 2010, IU released several songs that really pushed her singing career: "Nagging" (featuring 2AM's Lim Seul-ong) and "Because I Am A Woman" for the *Road No.1* K-drama OST.

In 2013, IU embarked on her first starring role in the K-drama *You're the Best, Lee Soon-Shin*. She had been in some other minor K-drama roles, but this was a huge feat considering the series went on for fifty episodes. Her next starring role was in 2015 in the drama *Producers*. It was a highly anticipated drama as she starred alongside top actors, Kim Soo-Hyun, Cha Tae-Hyun, and Gong Hyo-Jin. IU continued to get starring roles, including her role in the historical series *Moon Lovers: Scarlet Heart Ryeo* and *My Mister*.

IU is considered to be one of the most successful solo artists in South Korea, based on earnings. She has been nominated for and won many prestigious awards, including Lyricist of the Year and Producer of the Year at the 2018 Gaon Chart Music Awards, Digital Daesang and Bonsang at the 2018 Golden Disc Awards, and Album of the Year at the 2018 Melon Music Awards.

J

Jaurim

Jaurim is an indie rock band whose first huge single was titled "Hey Hey Hey." In 1999 and 2001, they won the Mnet Asian Music Award for Best Rock performance.

JBJ

A South Korean project boy band which included six members who were part of the second season of *Produce 101* in 2017. They debuted in October of 2017 and disbanded in April of 2018.

Jeong Se-Woon

Jeong Se-Woon was born on May 31, 1997. He is a singer-songwriter who is rose to fame after his appearance on the third season of the reality singing series *K-Pop Star*. Shortly after the show ended, he signed with the agency Starship Entertainment. In 2017, he found himself on another reality K-pop series titled

Produce 101. Impressively, he ranked 12th, meaning he had just missed the spot of getting to be a part of the group Wanna One.

On August 31, 2017, Jeong Se-Woon released his first EP, *Ever*, which did very well on the charts. That same year, he even won the Rising Star Award at the 2nd Asia Artist Awards. He has also made appearances on the variety shows *It's Dangerous Beyond the Blankets* and *Begin Again 2*.

Jessi

Jessi, whose full name is Jessica Hyun-Ju Ho, was born on December 17, 1988. She had moved to South Korea from New Jersey when she was fifteen years old in hopes of becoming a singer. In 2005, she debuted with a single album titled *Get Up* and performed her single on the music program *Music Bank*. After releasing her second single album, *The Rebirth*, in January of 2009, she took a break and went back to the U.S.

In 2014, Jessi returned to Korea and joined the hip-hop group Lucky J alongside J'Kyun and J-Yo. Jessi's big breakthrough came when she joined the rap reality series *Unpretty Rapstar* in January of 2015. She made it to the final two. After her appearance on the show, Jessi started to gain a lot of traction as she was featured on Park Jin-Young's single, "Who's Your Mama?" The song topped all the major charts and pushed Jessi to stardom.

In 2015, Jessi released her solo single titled "Sseununni" and in 2017, she released her EP, *Un2verse*, and promoted the single titled "Gucci."

Jinusean

When YG Entertainment opened its doors in 1996, Jinusean was the first K-pop group in which Yang Hyun Suk and YG Entertainment invested both their time and money. This amazing hip-hop duo consisted of Kim Jin-Woo (Jinu) and Noh Seung-Hwan (Sean). They were the first group that YG pushed into the K-pop scene and it is well known that Jinusean paved the way for the hip-hop genre into mainstream. Their first single was a megahit titled "Tell Me" featuring vocals from Uhm Jung-Hwa.

JJ Project

A sub-unit from the group GoT7, which includes members Jinyoung and JB. They released their first single in May of 2012, "Bounce."

Jjang/Zzang

The slang word referring to when something or someone is the best.
E.g., "The new Apink album is jjang!"

Jjim-jil-bang

Jjim-jil-bang is a place many South Koreans go to in order to relax and socialize. It contains several saunas with different degrees of heat. There is also a snack bar where you can get various types of delicious food and you can also play games and talk with friends while hanging out. There are a lot of K-pop idols and celebrities who visit jjim-jil-bangs on variety shows.

Jo Sung-Mo

Jo Sung-Mo was born on March 11, 1977. He is a solo singer who debuted in 1998 with the album *To Heaven*. Jo Sung-Mo became popular very quickly in the '90s upon the release of his album as his first single, also titled "To Heaven," was very well-received. The music video starred famous actor Lee Byung Hun and it followed a tragic love story.

On September 1, 1999, he released his second album, *For Your Soul*, which was also very successful. That same year, he won the Album Grand Prize and Album Main Prize at the Golden Disc Awards, Best Ballad Performance at the Mnet Asian Music Awards, and the New Artist Award at the Seoul Music Awards.

John Park

John Park was born on September 13, 1988. He had originally been a contestant on *American Idol*, but then ventured to Korea to partake in the Korean version of *American Idol* called *Superstar K 2*. He made it down to the final two on the program and signed with the label Music Farm Entertainment shortly after. On February 23, 2012, John Park released his first EP, *Knock*, and won the Best New Male Solo Artist Award at the 2nd Gaon Chart K-Pop Awards for the song "Falling." His first studio album, *Inner Child*, was released on July 3, 2013.

Jonh-daet-mal

The term used for speaking in formal Korean. This is a polite way of speaking to people you are meeting for the first time.

E.g., "We should keep using jonh-daet-mal because I'm not comfortable enough with you yet."

Joo

Joo, whose full name is Jung Min-Joo, was born on October 11, 1990. She was originally on the singing survivor show called *Superstar Survival* in 2006. After the show, she got accepted into JYP Entertainment and began her life as a trainee. In 2008, Joo made her solo debut with the single, "Young Girl," but after her debut, she felt she wasn't ready to step out into the spotlight, and instead, she went back to being a trainee.

Joo made her return on January 3, 2011 by uploading a video of her song on YouTube, which was off her EP, *Heartmade*. A few months later, she released a song and music video featuring Super Junior's Leeteuk titled "Ice Cream."

On January 2015, Joo's contract with JYP Entertainment came to an end and in April, she signed with Woollim Entertainment. She released her single, "Cry & Blow," later that year.

Jooyoung

Jooyoung was born on March 9, 1991 and debuted with a mini-album titled *From Me to You* in 2012. He was originally signed with the label RealCollabo, but then signed with Belikewater Records. In 2014, Jooyoung again signed with a different label, this time with Starship Entertainment. He collaborated with Hyolyn that same year for his first digital single release, "Erase."

Jooyoung enlisted into the military in November of 2015, and after being discharged, released a mini-album titled *Fountain*.

Jung Joon-Young

Jung Joon-Young was born on February 21, 1989. He spent a lot of time traveling when he was younger, as his father was an international businessman. He was born in Jakarta and has lived in Indonesia, China, Japan, France, and Philippines. Jung Joon-Young moved to Korea to start his music career. Although he had been in several different agencies, Jung Joon-Young's rise to fame came when was auditioned and became a contestant on *Superstar K* 4 in 2012. He performed a duet with Roy Kim on the show, which went on to achieve all-kill status.

Although Jung Joon-Young did not win the competition, he did make it to the final three. The show also provided several opportunities for him, as he was able to appear on some popular variety shows like *Immortal Songs*, *Happy Together*, *Radio Star*, *Law of the Jungle*, *Salty Tour*, and *We Got Married*. He's also been a set cast member on the show *2 Days & 1 Night* since 2013. Jung Joon-Young released his first studio album on February 7, 2017, *The First Person*.

Jung Seung-Hwan

Jung Seung-Hwan was born on August 21, 1996. He is known for being the runner-up on the fourth season of the singing elimination show *K-Pop Star*. Shortly after, he signed with the label Antenna and made his debut on November of 2016 with his EP, *His Voice*. His first studio album, *Spring Again*, was released on February 19, 2018.

Jungshook

"Jungshook" is a term used to describe being shocked or excited about something. It is a specific reference to whenever BTS's

Jungkook is in a state of shock. There were popular memes circulating online that started this term.

E.g., "Did you see BTS's new teaser for their album?" "Omonah, I'm jungshook."

Juniel

Juniel, who was born with the name Choi Jun-Hee, but is also known as Choi Seo-Ah, was born on September 3, 1993. She made her solo debut on April 29, 2011 with the release of a Japanese EP, *Ready Go*. Her South Korean debut came on June 7, 2012, when she released her single, "Illa Illa," followed by the release of her EP, *My First June*. That same year, she won the New Rising Star Award at the 27th Golden Disk Awards and the Rookie Singer Award at the 19th Korean Entertainment Arts Awards.

JYJ

A group that was formed in 2010 as a result of the disbandment of the K-pop group, TVXQ. Three of the members from TVXQ, Jaejoong, Yoochun, and Junsu, started their own group under C-JeS Entertainment and released their first record in Japanese.

JYP Entertainment

A company that was made by pop star Park Jin-young in 1997. It is considered to be one of the most successful music agencies in South Korea. Some famous K-pop groups who were previously with the agency were g.o.d, Rain, Jay Park, Wonder Girls, and Miss A. They are currently home to artists 2PM, Suzy, GoT7, DAY6, TWICE, and Stray Kids.

Kangnam

Kangnam, whose real name is Yasuo Namekawa, was born on March 23, 1987. He is a Korean Japanese singer who used to be part of the group M.I.B. Kangnam's rise to fame came when he appeared on the variety show *I Live Alone* in 2014. By the end of the year, he was hosting the SBS Gayo Daejun festival, which was a huge feat. While appearing on various variety shows throughout the years and winning awards for his appearance on them, Kangnam has released solo singles in Korea as well as Japan.

Kangta

Kangta, whose real name is Ahn Chil-Hyun, is better known for being part of the legendary boy group H.O.T. After the group disbanded, Kangta renewed his contract with SM Entertainment, and he made his solo debut, *Polaris*, in 2001. Since then, he has released several more albums and has also been actively producing various songs for himself and other K-pop artists.

Kara

Kara was a girl group which was formed in 2007 under DSP Media. The group's name comes from the Greek word "chara," which means "sweet melody." The original members of the group were Park Gyuri, Han Seung-Yeon, Kim Sung-Hee, and Nicole Jung. They debuted with their first album, *The First Blooming*, in March of 2007 and performed their single off the album "Break It" on *M Countdown*.

In March of 2008, Kim Sung-Hee announced that she would be leaving the group. In her place, Goo Ha-Ra and Kang Jiyoung joined the group. That same month, the group released their mini-album, *Rock U*. The success of Kara continued to rise with the release of several albums and singles. They won the Bonsang Award at the Seoul Music Awards in 2010 and 2012 as well as the Disc Bonsang at the Golden Disc Awards in 2012 and 2013.

On January of 2014, Nicole's contract with DSP came to an end, which caused her to depart from the group. Jiyoung also departed after her contract ended in April that same year. The remaining members continued to promote as Kara until July when Young-Ji joined the group through the reality TV show *Kara Project*. In January of 2016, Gyuri, Seungyeon, and Hara left the group after their contracts came to an end.

K.A.R.D

K.A.R.D is an acronym for the playing cards that each member represents: The King (K), Ace (A), Joker (R), and the hidden (D) card. The members are BM, J.Seph, Somin, and Jiwoo. Although their official debut was in July of 2017, they had released three songs prior to that, which included *K.A.R.D Project Vol.1* "Oh NaNa," "Don't Recall," and "Rumor."

Kasper

Kasper, whose real name is Lee Se-Rin, was born on April 17, 1993. She is a rapper who appeared as a contestant on both *Show Me the Money* 4 and *Unpretty Rapstar* 2. In 2016, Kasper signed with DSP Media and she made her debut on January 18, 2017, with the single, "Lean On Me."

Katie Kim

Katie Kim was born on December 10, 1993. She won first place on the singing show *K-Pop Star* 4. She signed with YG Entertainment and began training in preparation for her debut. After her contract ended, she joined another agency, AXIS, but YG continues to be in charge of the release of her debut album. In 2018, she released two singles, "Remember" and "Echo."

KBS Song Festival

The KBS Song Festival first started in 1965. It has gone through several changes, as it used to be an awards show, but currently, it is just a song festival where popular K-pop groups and artists perform.

K-Con

K-Con (Korean Convention) is a large music festival that was created in 2012 by Koreaboo. The artists are all from the K-pop

industry and the festival has spread worldwide since then. K-Con has been held in Dubai, Japan, France, Mexico, Australia, and all over the US.

Kenzie

Kenzie, whose real name is Kim Yeon-Jung, is a songwriter under SM Entertainment. She graduated from Berklee College of Music and found her way back to Korea where she was given the opportunity to work for SM Entertainment. To date, she has produced bestselling songs for K-pop groups and artists like, BoA, TVXQ, Super Junior, SHINee, Girls' Generation, f(x), EXO, and Red Velvet.

Kim Bum-Soo

Kim Bum-Soo was born on January 26, 1979, and is a popular ballad singer in South Korea. In 1999, he debuted with the album titled *A Promise*. Kim Bum-Soo is most known for his contribution to popular K-drama OSTs. His first big breakthrough was the song "I Miss You," on the *Stairway to Heaven* soundtrack.

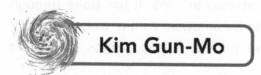

Kim Gun-Mo

Kim Gun-Mo was born on January 13, 1968 and is a legendary singer-songwriter. He debuted in 1992, but his bestselling album was his third, which was released on January 1, 1995, and titled *Wrongful Encounter*. It is considered to be one of the bestselling albums in Korea of all time.

Kim Jong-Kook

Kim Jong-Kook was born on April 25, 1976. He was originally a singer for the K-pop duo Turbo in the '90s. After the duo disbanded, he started his solo career, but it was his appearance on the popular variety show *X-Man* that maintained his popularity. In 2005, Kim Jong-Kook released his third album, *This Is Me*, which was a big success. Throughout his solo career, Kim Jong-Kook continued to rise in popularity and success through his variety show appearances. After *X-Man*, he appeared as a regular cast member for the show *Family Outing* (2008–2010) and then *Running Man* (2010–present).

Kim Jong-Kook's success as both a TV personality and solo artist has been outstanding. He has won several prestigious awards for both his involvement in variety shows and his career as a solo artist. In 2004, he won the Bonsang at the Seoul Music Awards and the Popularity Award at the Golden Disc Awards In 2005, his single, "Lovable," won him several awards at the MBC, KBS, and SBS Music Awards. That same year, he also managed to win the Bonsang Award at the Golden Disk Awards and Best Male Artist at the Mnet Asian Music Awards. His variety show appearances have won him several awards throughout the years at the SBS and KBS Entertainment Awards.

Kim Kyung-Ho

Kim Kyung-Ho was born on June 7, 1971. He debuted in 1995 with his self-titled album, *Kim Kyung Ho*. He is best known for his high vocal range and his catchy rock songs. He has earned the title of being a rock legend and has continued to release music while appearing on popular variety shows.

Kim Yeon-Woo

Kim Yeon-Woo was born on July 22, 1971. He sang alongside Yoo Hee-Yeol's band, Toy, and they went on to produce the hit songs "Still Beautiful" and "Remember I Was Next to You" that are considered classics today. After his time with Toy, he released several solo albums and appeared on various variety shows that brought him more popularity. He is known for his flawless and smooth singing abilities as well as high vocal range.

King of Mask Singer

King of Mask Singer is a popular music program that is hosted by Kim Sung-Joo. The show's premise involves guest celebrities appearing in a full mask and costume in front of a live audience as well as a panel of cast members. The guest celebrity sings several songs and the panel must try and figure out which popular celebrity is behind the mask. These celebrities range from being famous K-pop idols to actors/actresses and even comedians. The show's success has even brought a US version of the show.

KittiB

KittiB, whose real name is Kim Bo-Mi, was born on July 27, 1990. She became well-known after her appearance as a contestant on the rapping competition show Unpretty Rapstar 2. Although she didn't win first place, she was the runner-up and was able to sign with the label Brand New Music shortly after.

KNK

KNK is a boy group that was formed under YNB Entertainment and debuted in 2016. There are five members in the group: Youjin, Seungjun, Inseong, Jihun, and Heejun. They released their first single, "Knock," in March 2016.

Koreaboo

Koreaboo is the term used to reference someone who is really fascinated and interested in the South Korean culture. The person can be obsessed with K-pop, video games, K-dramas, or the language and culture in general.

E.g., "I'm obsessed with South Korean pop culture! I love everything about it!"

"You should go visit in the summer or something."

"Oh, I totally am. I've already got my flight booked!"

"You're such a koreaboo!"

Korean Music Awards

The Korean Music Awards is a ceremony that recognizes mainstream and independent music artists. The awards are given based on record sales and the opinions of a panel of judges. There are about twenty categories in the ceremony and the main one is Musician of the Year. In 2018, the winner of this particular award was given to BTS. The previous year, it was given to Jay Park.

Koyote

Koyote is a co-ed K-pop group that originated in 1998. The original members were Shinji, Kim Goo, and Cha Seung Min. Their first single, "Innocent," was released in 1998 and it became a huge hit, mainly for its catchy and upbeat melody. There were many members who left and joined the group, but the ones who remain today are Shinji, Kim Jong Min, and Baekja.

K-Tigers

K-Tigers is a group of taekwondo athletes who specialize in demonstrating cool tricks to big audience. They also upload videos on YouTube, incorporating videos that combine taekwondo with dance to popular K-pop songs.

Kwak Jin-Eon

Kwak Jin-Eon was born on October 23, 1991. He is best known for having won first place on the singing competition show *Superstar K 6* in 2014. His first album, which was titled *Go With Me*, was released in May of 2016.

K.Will

K.Will, whose real name is Kim Hyung-Soo, was born on December 30, 1981. K.Will was first signed to Big Hit Entertainment, but then signed with Starship Entertainment in 2008. He has released four studio albums, six EPs, and several singles that have all done well on the charts. He is also known for being the voice of some popular OST songs. Some popular dramas that he has sung on the OST for include "Like a Star" for the drama *My Love from the Star*, "Talk Love" for *Descendants of the Sun*, and "Melting" for *Love in the Moonlight*.

LABOUM

LABOUM, which means "party" in French, is a girl group that debuted in 2014. It has members Yujeong, Soyeon, ZN, Haein, and Solbin. Yulhee was originally part of the group, but she left the group in 2017. They released their first single album, *Petit Macaron*, in 2014 and launched their music video for the song "Pit-A-Pat."

Ladies' Code

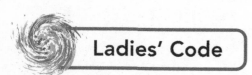

Signed under Polaris Entertainment in 2013, Ladies' Code debuted in March of 2013. The original members of the group were Ashley, Sojung, Zuny, EunB, and RiSe. On September 3, 2014, the group was in a tragic car accident that resulted in the deaths of EunB and RiSe. Two years later, the group returned as a trio.

Law of the Jungle

Law of the Jungle is a television series that airs on SBS every Friday. It takes a group of K-pop idols and other celebrities to a remote jungle that could be anywhere in the world. This group is forced to survive on their own, hunting for their own food and making their own shelter. The creator and main cast member of the show is the comedian Kim Byung-Man. There have been many famous K-pop idols featured on the show such as ZE:A's HWang Kwanghee, SHINee's Onew, Teen Top's Niel, EXO's Chanyeol, GOT7's Jackson, EXID's Hani, VIXX's N, and AOA's Seolhyun. It has proven to be quite successful and has been on air since 2011.

Leader

In almost every K-pop group, there is a designated leader. The leaders tend to be chosen by the company and are usually the oldest members in the group. Sometimes the title is given to the member with the most experience or the member who signed with the company first.

Lee Hi

Lee Hi was born on September 23, 1996. She was the runner-up on the first season of the singing competition show *K-Pop Star* in 2012. She signed with YG Entertainment after the show and on October of that year, she released the single "1, 2, 3, 4." On March 28, 2013, Lee Hi released her debut album, *First Love*. On March 9, 2016, Lee Hi released her album, *Seoulite*, through Tablo's label, HIGHGRND. She promoted the singles "Breathe" (written by SHINee's Jonghyun) and "My Star." Her song "Breathe" was a big success and it even won the Digital Bonsang at the Golden Disk Awards in 2017.

Lee Juck

Lee Juck was born on February 28, 1974. He was originally part of the group Panic in the '90s, but is now a solo singer. He has made several appearances on popular variety shows and has released several solo albums over the years. He's also known for the song "Don't Worry," that he sang on the *Reply 1988* K-drama, for which he won the Best OST Award at the Mnet Asian Music Awards in 2016.

Lee Moon-Se

Lee Moon Se was born on January 17, 1959. He is a singer-songwriter and is considered to be one of the most respected South Korean singers in the industry. His albums have topped charts and have become bestsellers. He also won the Grand Prize at the Golden Disk Awards in 1987.

Lee Seung-Chul

Lee Seung-Chul was born on December 6, 1966. He was the main vocalist of the rock band Boohwal until he decided to become a solo artist. His first album was titled *Don't Say Goodbye*. In 2009, Lee Seung Chul became a judge on the popular singing competition show *Superstar K*. He stepped down as a judge in 2014.

Lee Seung-Hwan

Lee Seung Hwan was born on December 13, 1965. He is a famous singer and producer in the Korean music industry. He debuted in 1989 with the release of his album, *B.C 604*. He became known for his ballad songs.

Lee So-Ra

Lee So-Ra is a singer who was originally part of the group Strange People. She debuted in 1993 with the group, but then released a solo album on September 1, 1995 titled *Lee So-Ra Vol. 1*. Since then, she released seven more albums and hosted a music show called *Lee Sora's Proposal* from 1996 to 2002.

Lee Soo Man

Lee Soo Man is the founder of SM Entertainment, which is one of the largest entertainment companies in South Korea. He founded SM in 1989 and was a pioneer for starting the Hallyu wave.

Leessang

A hip-hop duo that included members Gary and Gil, formed in 2002. To date, they have released eight albums and many chart-topping singles that have remained classics. Gary is also internationally well-known for his previous role on the variety show *Running Man*.

Lexy

Lexy, whose real name is Hwang Hyo-Sook, was born on May 3, 1977. She signed under YG Entertainment in 2003 and was the first female rap artist that the label had signed. Lexy was featured on several songs with fellow YG artists, Se7en, 1TYM, Jinusean, and Wheesung. She released her first album on October 6, 2003, *LEXURY*. In 2007, Lexy and YG Entertainment parted ways and she signed with SB&W Entertainment.

Liners

The term used when there are K-pop idols or celebrities who share the same year of birth. They refer to the year they were born and then add the word "liners" after it.

E.g., "The '88 liners, G-Dragon, Taeyang, and Kwanghee, are releasing a song together!"

"I know, I'm so excited!"

Loco

Loco, whose real name is Kwon Hyuk-Woo, was born on December 25, 1989. He is a rapper who is signed under Jay Park's label, AOMG. Loco rose to fame when he won first place in the first season of the rap competition series *Show Me the Money* in 2012. He has released several singles in collaboration with other popular K-pop idols and artists, such as Crush, Eric Nam, Sam Kim, Hwasa, and Jung Yong Hwa. He released two EPs, *Locomotive* (November 2014) and *Summer Go Loco* (August 2017), and one studio album, *Bleached* (May 2017).

Loona

When Loona first debuted, they were introduced to the public in the revealing of one member every month. From October 2016 to January 2017, members Heejin, Hyunjin, Haseul, and Yeojin were revealed. Between April and July, ViVi, Kim Lip, JinSoul, and Choerry were revealed. And finally, from November to January of 2018, Yves, Chuu, and Go Won were introduced. Olivia Hye was the final member to be revealed in March of 2018.

There were three sub-units formed within the group. The first sub-unit formed was with members Heejin, Hyunjin, Haseul, and ViVi. They were named Loona 1/3 . The second sub-unit was named Loona Odd Eye Circle with members JinSoul, Kim Lip, and Cheorry. The final and third sub-unit, Loona yyxy, included members Yves, Chuu, Go Won, and Olivia Hye.

Love call

Love call is the term used when K-pop idols or celebrities are in "high demand," meaning they are wanted on variety shows, commercials, K-dramas, or other entertainment outlets because of their charm.

Loveleyz

Loveleyz was formed in 2014 by Woollim Entertainment. The eight-member girl group includes members Baby Soul, Jiae, Jisoo, Mijoo, Kei, Jin, Sujeong, and Yein. They released their first album in November of 2014, titled *Girls' Invasion*.

Lunafly

Lunafly is a group who debuted under Nega Network. The original members included Teo, Sam, and Yun. They debuted their first single in 2012 along with the music video for the song "How Nice Would It Be." Their second single, "Clear Day, Cloudy Day," was released in December of 2012. In 2014, the group went on a Latin American tour, visiting Mexico, Guatemala, Peru, Brazil, and Costa Rica. They also went on a European and Canadian tour. In the midst of these tours, Teo left Lunafly and Jin and Yub were added to the group.

Lyn

Lyn was born on November 9, 1981. She is a popular singer who has been active since 2001. She had released an album under her real name, Lee Se-Jin, but the album failed to be successful, so she took some time off and came back in 2002, changing her stage name to Lyn. Her first album was titled *Have You Ever Had a Broken Heart?* People loved her vocals and R&B genre, which pushed her into the spotlight and put her on the map. The next few albums she released were also very successful and she had established herself as a respected singer in the industry.

Lyn also began to sing for various K-drama OSTs that were big hits. Her most recognizable song was for the hit K-drama *My Love from the Star*, which was titled "My Destiny." For this particular song alone, she won six awards in 2014, including Best OST at the 50th Baeksang Arts Awards, Outstanding Korean Drama OST at the 9th Seoul International Drama Awards, Best OST at the 6th Melon Music Awards, and Best OST at the 16th Mnet Asian Music Awards.

M Countdown

A music program on Mnet that airs every Thursday evening. K-pop singers and groups go on the show to perform the songs that they are promoting.

Mad Clown

Mad Clown, whose real name is Jo Dong-Rim, was born on March 25, 1985. He is a rapper and producer signed under Starship Entertainment. He debuted with the single "Luv Sickness" and appeared on the rap competition series *Show Me The Money* as a contestant in season two and then a producer and judge in season 5.

MADTOWN

A seven-member boy group that was formed in 2014 by J. Tune Camp. The members of MADTOWN were Moos, Daewoon, Lee Geon, Jota, Heo Jun, Buffy, and H.O. They made their debut with their album, *Mad Town*, in October of 2014. In November of 2017, the group revealed that they were in the early stages of disbandment as a result of their agency closing down.

Maht-hyung

Term that refers to the oldest male in the group.

Mak-choom

The term used to describe a type of dance that is totally random and un-choreographed. "Mak" means "random" and "choom" means "dance" in Korean. A lot of K-pop idols and stars are asked to do this type of dance on variety shows as it is entertaining and funny.

Maknae

The endearing term for the youngest member of a group. The youngest members usually have the image of being cute and innocent, but obviously this is not always the case!

MAMAMOO

Formed by RBW in 2014, members of MAMAMOO include Solar, Moonbyul, Wheein, and Hwasa. They debuted in June of 2014 with the song "Mr. Ambiguous" from their album *Hello*. The music video for "Mr. Ambiguous" became popular very quickly as it featured appearances from many other K-pop idols and singers.

MBC Gayo Daejeon

MBC Gayo Daejeon is a year-end music special that showcases various K-pop groups and artists. It is organized by Munhwa Broadcasting Company (MBC).

MBLAQ

MBLAQ stands for "Music Boys Live in Absolutely Quality." They were created by the K-pop star Rain under the company J. Tune Camp. The members include Seungho, G.O, Mir, Lee Joon, and Thunder, but Lee Joon and Thunder left the group in December of 2014.

MC Mong

MC Mong, whose real name is Shin Dong-Hyun, was born on September 4, 1979. He was a hip-hop artist and TV personality who became popular in the early 2000s. He was an actor on the popular sitcom series *Nonstop*, which helped him with his career. In 2004, he released his first album, *180 Degree*. He also became a fixed cast member on the show *2 Days & 1 Night* from 2007–2010.

ME U

ME U is the official name of the fan club for f(x). They announced the name of their fan club at the group's first solo concert in 2016.

Melodies

Melodies is what BtoB calls their fans. Because their group name means "Born to Beat," they decided that the best thing that goes with a beat is the melody, which is why they gave their fans the name.

Melody Day

Melody Day is a girl group that was formed in 2012 under Cre.ker Entertainment. The original members were Yeoeun, Chahee, and Yein. They released their single album, *Another Parting*, in February of 2014 and then in October of 2014, Yoomin was added to the group. The first song they released as a four-member group was "Listen to My Heart" for the *Naeil's Cantabile* OST. Their first mini-album, *Color*, was released on July 1, 2016.

Melon Music Awards

The Melon Music Awards is an awards ceremony that is held every year. Melon is an online music store where people can purchase songs and albums from their favorite K-pop artists and groups. The awards are distributed based on various factors such as online voting, digital sales, and judges' scores. The main awards are Artist of the Year, Album of the Year, and Song of the Year.

M.I.B

Otherwise known as "Most Incredible Busters," M.I.B was a four-member hip-hop group formed under Jungle Entertainment. Members of the group were 5Zic, Young Cream, SIMS, and Kangnam. The group disbanded in January of 2017.

Mini album

Mini albums tend to have only a few songs. Whereas a full album would have about twelve songs or more, a mini-album can have anywhere from four to six.

Miss A

Miss A was signed under JYP Entertainment in 2010. The group members included Fei, Jia, Min, and Suzy. They made their official debut with the song "Bad Girl Good Girl," which was a huge hit. The song won first place on KBS *Music Bank*, which was impressive considering it was the first song they released. Jia and Min left the group before the group officially disbanded in December of 2017.

MIX & MATCH

A survival program created by YG Entertainment in 2014. The show's purpose was to form a boy group, which resulted in the creation of the group iKon.

MIXNINE

A reality music show made by YG Entertainment. The founder of YG, Yang Hyung Suk, traveled to other music companies and recruited potential K-pop stars. There was a final round of nine boys and nine girls with the winning team debuting as a group. Due to a conflict in contracts, the final group was unable to debut.

Mnet Asian Music Awards

The Mnet Asian Music Awards, which is also known as MAMA, is an awards ceremony put on annually by CJ E&M. The first ceremony was held in Seoul, South Korea in 1999, but since 2011, it has been held in various countries. The big awards are Album of the Year, Song of the Year, and Artist of the Year.

MOBB

A hip-hop unit formed by YG Entertainment in 2016. MOBB included members Mino from Winner and Bobby from iKon. Bobby had gained a lot of popularity as he had won first place in the third season of the rap reality show *Show Me the Money*. Mino had also gained success as he won second place the following year on the same show.

The duo debuted with their EP titled *The Mobb*.

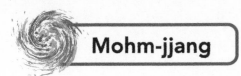

Mohm-jjang

The term referring to someone who has a really nice body. Literal translation is "body-the best."

Mol-ca

A slang term for hidden camera. In South Korea, they love to pull hidden camera pranks on celebrities and air them on television.

Momoland

Momoland was formed through the reality show *Finding Momoland*. The finalists of the show became members of the group: Hyebin, Yeonwoo, Jane, Nayun, JooE, Ahin, and Nancy. Daisy and Taeha were added later on. The group was signed under MLD Entertainment and they debuted in November of 2016. Their first EP was titled *Welcome to Momoland*.

MONBEBE

MONBEBE is the name that MONSTA X gave their fans. They had explained that their group name means "My star" so they thought "My baby" would be a good fit for their fans.

MONSTA X

MONSTA X was formed through the Mnet show *No.Mercy* in 2015. They signed under Starship Entertainment and debuted in May of 2015. The members in MONSTA X include Shownu, Wonho, Minhyuk, Kihyun, Hyungwon, Jooheon, and I.M. The group is known for their powerful choreography and strong visuals.

Monster Rookie

The term used for groups who became successful very quickly. An example of a group who quickly gained success is BLACKPINK.

MooMoos

Fans of MAMAMOO are called MooMoos. In Korean, the word "Moo" means "radish," which is why their official lightstick is in the shape of one.

Mukbang

Mukbang is the term used for people who display their eating habits on TV or online. There are lots of famous K-pop idols and celebrities who are known to be great at showing their eating abilities. Some famous "mukbang idols" include MAMAMOO's Hwasa and Highlight's Yoon Doo-Joon.

Music Bank

A music program that airs every Friday on KBS2 in South Korea. Many K-pop idols and artists perform on stage with a live audience in this show.

MV

The short version of "music video."

MXM

MXM is a K-pop duo consisting of members Im Young-Min and Kim Dong-Hyun. They are a sub-unit duo from the group Brand New Boys, who are under the label Brand New Music. They both participated in season 2 of *Produce 101*, but neither of them made it to the final group, Wanna One. MXM officially debuted on September 6, 2017 with their EP, *Unmix*. Their second EP, *Match Up*, was released on January 10, 2018.

MyDOL

MyDOL was a reality show that followed the process of VIXX becoming a group. Ten trainees under Jellyfish Entertainment had to complete various tasks and missions to get through to the finals to become a part of the final six-member group. The show premiered on April 12, 2012. The final group performed on *M Countdown* on May 24, 2012.

Myeong-dong

Myeong-dong is a specific area in the heart of Seoul that attracts a lot of tourists, mainly because it's a shopping haven to pick up Korean beauty products as well as K-pop merchandise. The area has mass amounts of vendors and stores that are dedicated to posters, calendars, key chains, cell phone cases, and other swag you can get of your favorite K-pop group or idol.

MYNAME

MYNAME was formed by Fly to the Sky's Hwanhee under H2 Media. The members are Gunwoo, Insoo, Seyong, JunQ, and Chaejin. The group debuted in October of 2011 and has released six albums since then.

Mystic Entertainment

Mystic Entertainment is an entertainment label that was founded by singer-songwriter Yoon Jong-Shin. The label was founded in 2001. Some popular artists under the label include Uhm Jung-Hwa, Eddy Kim, and Brown Eyed Girls.

MYTEEN

MYTEEN is a boy group under The Music Works label. They debuted in 2017 with the release of their EP titled *MYTEEN GO!* The members of the group are Lee Taevin, Chunjin, Eunsu, Kim Kookheon, Shin Junseop, Song Yuvin, and Hanseul. Their second EP, titled *F;UZZLE*, was released on July 10, 2018.

Naver

Naver is an online platform that is operated in South Korea. It is the most used search engine in South Korea. On this platform, K-pop fans can see which of their favorite artists are topping the charts and also get the latest news on any celebrity.

NCT

NCT stands for "Neo Culture Technology." The founder of the group, SM Entertainment, went with the concept of having an unlimited number of members in this boy group, which is why there are so many sub-units within NCT.

The first sub-unit that was made was called NCT U. They made their debut with the single "The 7th Sense." The second unit was NCT 127 and they released a mini-album titled *NCT #127*. The third unit, NCT Dream, came out with the single "Chewing Gum" in August of 2016. There are currently eighteen members in total.

Netizens

The term used to describe the online community of people who like to bully. It is a community of people that is feared by many and are likely to be harsh on famous people, especially K-pop idols.

N.Fia

The name of the fandom for N.Flying. It is a combination of the name of their group and the word "utopia."

N.Flying

A group that is under FNC Entertainment, N.Flying is a rap rock band who was formed in 2013. The members include Lee Seung-Hyub, Kwon Kwang-Jin, Cha Hun, Kim Jae-Hyun, and Yoo Hwe-Seung. They released their first single, "Basket in Japan," in 2013.

Nine Muses

Nine Muses is a girl group that was formed under Star Empire Entertainment in 2010. Their concept is that the members would be able to graduate and new members would be admitted into the group. The current members of the group are Sungah, Kyungri, Hyemi, Sojin, and Keumjo.

Nine Muses A

A sub-unit group of Nine Muses, which includes members Kyungri, Hyemi, Sojin, and Keumjo. They released the single "Muses Diary" in August of 2016.

Noona

The term used from a male to an older female. They can be actual siblings or just have a close relationship.

Noona Killer

When there is a younger K-pop idol or celebrity who is capable of making the older women fall in love with his charm, he is referred to as a "noona killer."

E.g., "Did you see Cha Eun Woo winking while he danced?! He's such a noona killer!"

Noraebang

The Korean term for karaoke. The literal meaning is "singing room." In South Korea, noraebangs are a very common activity and are everywhere. You rent out a private room for however many hours and sing songs with your friends, colleagues, or even by yourself!

NRG

NRG, which stands for "New Radiancy Group," is a K-pop music group that included members Chun Myung-Hoon, Lee Sung-Jin, Noh Yoo-Min, Moon Sung-Hoon, and Kim Hwan-Sung. They debuted in 1997 and took several hiatuses until now, but have recently regrouped for their 20th debut anniversary. For the comeback, there were three active members: Chun Myung-Hoon, Lee Sung-Jin, and Noh Yoo-Min.

NS Yoon-Ji

NS Yoon-Ji, whose real name is Kim Yoon-Ji, was born on September 6, 1988. The "NS" in her name means "New Spirit." She debuted was originally a trainee under DSP Media, but then debuted under JTM Entertainment in 2009 with the single "Head Hurts." She has released many singles featuring several popular artists including Jay Park, Verbal Jint, DinDin, Giriboy, and MC Mong. Her first EP, *New Spirit*, was released on January 5, 2012.

NU'EST

Formed under Pledis Entertainment, NU'EST stands for "New Establish Style Tempo." The group members are JR, Aron, Baekho, Minhyun, and Ren. They debuted in March of 2012 with the song "Face." Min Hyun participated in the survival reality music program *Produce 101* and made it to the final eleven members, which formed the group Wanna One.

Nugu group

Nugu group is the term that refers to a K-pop group or artist that has not quite made it yet. It is considered to be a negative term. The direct translation of the word "nugu" in Korean is "who?"

OH MY GIRL

OH MY GIRL debuted in April of 2015 under WM Entertainment. They debuted with members Hyojung, Mimi, YooA, Seunghee, Jiho, Binnie, Arin, and JinE, but JinE departed from the group in 2017. Their first release was their mini-album, *Oh My Girl*, with the title song "Cupid." They have been nominated for several awards, but won the Best New Female Artist Award for the SBS Power FM Cultwo Show in 2015.

Omona/Omo

A word of expression that conveys either shock or surprise.

E.g., "Did you hear? BTS is doing a world tour and they're stopping in Toronto!"

"Omona! This is a once in a lifetime chance. We have to go!!!"

Once

Once is the term used to refer to the fandom of girl group TWICE.

ONE

ONE, whose real name is Jung Jae-Won, was born on March 29, 1994. He debuted in 2015 in the group 1Punch with Samuel Kim. They released the album *The Anthem*. However, ONE made his mark in the industry with his appearance on the fourth and fifth season of the rap competition series *Show Me the Money*. Although he didn't make it to the finals in either season, he got recruited from YG Entertainment, which meant he would no longer be part of 1Punch.

On July 11 2017, ONE debuted with his EP titled *One Day*. He is also pursuing an acting career as he made several appearances on various dramas like *Hwayugi* and *Anthology*, and is expected to be in the new TVN drama, *Room Nine*.

100%

100% is a boy group who was formed under TOP Media in 2012. The original members of the group were Rockhyun, Minwoo, Jonghwan, Hyukjin, Chanyong, Sanghoon, and Changbum. They released their first EP, *Real 100%*, on May 23, 2013.

In March 2014, Minwoo enlisted into the army and Sanghoon decided to step away from the spotlight. The remaining five members released their second EP, *Bang the Bush*, on March 17, 2014.

On September 12, 2016, Changbum decided to leave the group and the group released their third EP the following month, *Time Leap*. On March 25, 2018, Minwoo suddenly passed away.

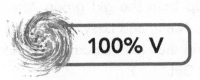

100% V

100% V is a sub-unit group of the group 100% consisting of members Rockhyun, Jonghwan, Hyukjin, and Chanyoung. They released the single "Missing You" on October 20, 2013.

ONF

This seven-member boy group signed under WM Entertainment in 2017. They debuted in August of 2017 with the song "ON/OFF." Members of the group include Hyojin, E-Tion, J-Us, Wyatt, MK, U, and Laun.

In 2017, the whole group auditioned for the survival music program *Mix Nine* where they all passed the first round. Hyojin and Laun made it to the final group, but were unable to debut as the project got cancelled. However, in 2018, ONF released their EP, *You Complete Me*, and music video for their song, "Complete."

Oppa

Oppa is the term used for when a younger female is addressing an older male. If they are close and comfortable with each other, it is considered a term of endearment. It is also the term used when they are blood related.

Orange Caramel

Orange Caramel is a sub-unit group from the girl group After School. The members include Raina, Nana, and Lizzy. The group debuted on June of 2010 by releasing their mini-album, *The First Mini Album*, and their single, "Magic Girl."

There was a warm response for this sub-unit group as they won several awards, some of which include Best Comic Video for their song "Lipstick," Most Underrated Girl Group for the Billboard's Girl Group Week, The Women CM Star Award for the MTN Broadcast Advertising Award Ceremony, and the Photogenic Award for the Korean Visual Arts Festival.

Orbit

In July of 2018, before their debut, Loona announced their official fandom name "Orbit" on Instagram through video.

Oricon

Oricon is a music chart in Japan. It consists of data from various outlets, sales, and other entertainment-based products. The results of the chart are announced every Tuesday.

OST

A shorter way of saying "Original Soundtrack." OSTs are usually released with K-dramas and movies, and have a good chance at being chart-toppers, especially if the K-drama/movie is a good one.

Paloalto

Paloalto, whose real name is Jeon Sang-Hyun, was born on January 24, 1984. He is a rapper and founder of the label Hi-Lite Records. His first EP, titled *Footprints*, was released on February 2, 2004. He is also known for his appearance on the fourth season of *Show Me the Money*.

Park Hyo Shin

A famous South Korean singer who is signed under Glove Entertainment. Park Hyo Shin gained popularity very quickly after debuting and even won the Rookie of the Year Award at the Golden Disk Awards in 2000. He has had many chart-topping songs, including "Snow Flower," "Memories Are Getting Similar to Love," "After Love," and "Wild Flower."

Park Ji-Yoon

Park Ji-Yoon was born on January 3, 1982. She is a singer who debuted as a model when she was thirteen years old. She signed with JYP Entertainment and released her first album in 1997, *Skyblue Dream*. After releasing her sixth album, she left JYP Entertainment. Park Ji-Yoon left the spotlight for six years until she made a comeback under Sony Music Korea with her seventh album, *Flower, Again for the First Time*.

In 2013, she left Sony Music Korea and signed with Mystic89. After a few years, she started her own label called Park Ji Yoon Creative. On March 2, 2017, she released her ninth album, *Park Ji Yoon 9*.

Park Jin-young

Otherwise known as J.Y. Park or JYP, he is the founder of JYP Entertainment, one of the largest music entertainment companies in Korea. Before he was the founder of JYP Entertainment, he was a singer, releasing his first album in 1994, *Blue City*, with the song "Don't Leave Me," which was very well received in the public. Just a few years later, in 1997, he started up his agency, JYP Entertainment. His first project idol group was g.o.d, who took a couple years to debut, but when they finally did, they became one of the most popular K-pop groups at that time. Because Park Jin-young produced their songs, his reputation and image rose in the public eye. From this point on, Park Jin-young continued to produce megahits for various artists, including some American artists like Will Smith, Mase, and Cassie.

Park Jung Hyun

Park Jung Hyun, who also goes by Lena Park, is a singer who debuted in 1988. She was born in Los Angeles, California, but ventured to South Korea to embark on her dreams of becoming a singer. Her first album, *Piece*, was released in 1998. She had several songs on the album that were huge successes, including "P.S. I Love You" and a duet with Yim Jae-Bum titled "A Wound Deeper Than Love."

Since then, Park Jung-Hyun has continued to release several chart-topping albums and singles, and has sung the OST for many popular K-dramas.

Pentagon

Pentagon debuted in 2016 under Cube Entertainment. The group members are Jinho, Hui, Hongseok, E'Dawn, Shinwon, Yeo One, Yan An, Yuto, Kino, and Wooseok. They released their EP titled *Pentagon* on October of 2016 with the title song "Gorilla." They held their first concert on December of 2016 and were sold out immediately. Although fairly new, Pentagon was able to win the New Star Award at the Asia Model Awards and the New Artist of the Year Award at the Soribada Best K-Music Awards.

Pepero Day

Pepero Day is a day that is celebrated in South Korea on November 11. The eleventh month and the eleventh day all look like Pepero snacks, which are shaped like sticks. The purpose of Pepero Day is to buy this snack for friends, family, and lovers to show how much they mean to you. A lot of K-pop groups and artists partake in Pepero advertisements or fun social media posts to show their support of this day.

Please Take Care of My Refrigerator

Please Take Care of My Refrigerator is a cooking variety show that is aired on JTBC. It is a show where guests bring their refrigerators on the show and a panel of famous chefs cook up some gourmet meals for the guests using only the ingredients in their fridge. A lot of K-pop idols have made guest appearances on this show and have expressed their love and desire to be on it.

Point choreography

Point choreography is determined when there is a specific dance move in the song that sticks out, is repeated throughout, or people can follow along to. This part of the choreography is usually at the chorus of a song.

Primadonna

Primadonna is the name that F.T. Island gave their fans. It is signifi-cant to them as it is a song title off their first album, *Cheerful Sensibility*.

Primary

Primary, whose real name is Choi Dong Hoon, is a popular hip-hop musician as well as record producer. He has produced albums for Dynamic Duo and MBLAQ.

Pristin

Pristin is a ten-member girl group that was formed under Pledis Entertainment in 2016. The members of Pristin are Nayoung, Roa, Yuha, Eunwoo, Rena, Kyulkyung, Yehana, Sungyeon, Xiyeon, and Kyla. Before the debut of this group, Nayoung, Roya, Yuha, Eunwoo, Rena, Kyulkyung, and Xiyeon all participated in the reality music program *Produce 101* in 2016. Nayoung and Kyulkyung made it to the finals and were able to debut with the group I.O.I in May of 2016.

On March of 2017, Pristin made their debut with the release of their mini-album, *Hi! Pristin*, with the title track "Wee Woo." They have gained a lot of success and have won several awards; they won the Rookie Award at the Asia Artist Awards, Best New Female Artist Award at the Mnet Asian Music Awards, New Artist Award at the Seoul Music Awards, and the Global Rookie Top 5 award at the V Live Awards.

Pristin V

Pristin V is a sub-unit group of Pristin that was formed in 2018. The members are Nayoung, Roa, Eunwoo, Rena, and Kyulkyung. They made their first release as a sub-unit with the single album *Like a V* with the single "Get It."

Produce 101

A reality survivor music program directed by Ahn Joon Young. There have been two seasons of this reality show in South Korea. It consists of gathering trainees from various agencies around South Korea to form a group who will be promoting together for a couple years. After the contract is done, the finalists will return to their agencies and/or groups.

The first season of *Produce 101* involved all females. There were 101 competitors and South Korea voted week after week for their favorite girls until there were only eleven left. The final eleven became the girl group I.O.I.

The second season of *Produce 101* had all male contestants. There were 101 trainees and the public chose their final eleven members. These members went on to become the group Wanna One.

Produce 48

Produce 48 aired in June of 2018 every Friday for twelve episodes. It is a reality survivor music show that airs on Mnet. It brings together ninety-six girls (from South Korea and Japan) who are still training to debut in their respective agencies and/or groups. The final twelve contestants are chosen through a voting system and those who make it to the finals will go on to promote as a group for two and a half years. The director of this program is Ahn Joon Young, who also directed *Produce 101*.

PSY

PSY, whose real name is Park Jae-Sang, was born on December 31, 1977. He is a producer and singer who is known for his international hit song, "Gangnam Style." Despite the fact that many people know him through the success of this particular song, PSY has been a singer in South Korea since 2001. After attending college in the United States for a brief period of time, PSY returned to Korea and debuted with his first album in January of 2001, *PSY from the PSYcho World!* He quickly became known for his inappropriate lyrics as well as quirky dance moves.

In 2010, PSY signed with YG Entertainment and he released his fifth album, *PSYFive*, that same year. However, his big breakthrough came in July of 2012 when he released his sixth album, *PSY 6*, which featured "Gangnam Style." At first, PSY was reluctant to release the music video for the song, but decided to do so on a whim. It quickly became first on YouTube's Most Viewed Videos monthly chart and on August 21, 2012, it was number one on the iTunes Music Video Charts.

The success of "Gangnam Style" gave him an opportunity to sign with Scooter Braun's record label, Schoolboy Records. He also performed and made appearances on various United States television shows like *The Today Show*, *Saturday Night Live*, and *Ellen*. PSY has since released two more albums, *Chilijip PSY-da* in December of 2015 and *4x2=8* in May of 2017. A year after the release of his eighth album, PSY left YG Entertainment.

Queen's

Queen's is the name for T-ara's fandom. It is a reference to T-ara being the queens and their fans belonging to them.

Radio Star

Radio Star is a talk show that has aired since May of 2007. Two of the four original hosts have remained on the show, Yoon Jong-Shin and Kim Gu-Ra. The other two original hosts, Shin Jung-Hwan and Shindong, departed from the show.

A lot of famous K-pop idols and stars appear on the show. The hosts discuss a lot of personal topics and rumors with the guests. It is known to be a platform where K-pop stars and celebrities can clear any misunderstandings or groundless rumors.

Rain

Rain, whose real name is Jung Ji-Hoon, was born on June 25, 1982. He is a trifecta in that he sings, acts, and produces music. He was originally a singer and signed with JYP, debuting with the group Fanclub. They released two albums, but failed to succeed. In 2002, Rain debuted as a solo artist with the album, *Bad Guy*, which was a success. He released his second album, *Rain 2*, and the title track "Ways to Avoid the Sun" was a huge success.

Rain's rise to fame continued as he became a bestselling artist all over Asia, which led to being recognized in 2006 by *Time* magazine in the United States as one of the 100 Most Influential People Who Shape Our World.

In November of 2007, Rain left JYP Entertainment to start his own label, J. Tune Entertainment. In December of 2009, J. Tune Entertainment merged with JYP Entertainment.

On October 16, 2008, Rain released his fifth album, *Rainism*, and he promoted the singles "Love Story" and "Rainism." The choreography for "Rainism" still continues to be covered by many popular K-pop idols today.

Rain made his K-drama debut in 2003 with the drama *Sang Doo! Let's Go To School*, but his real success as an actor came in 2004 when he starred in the romantic comedy *Full House* alongside Song Hye-Kyo. The drama was an international success, which earned him the title of being a Hallyu star. He starred in a few other dramas before he made his Hollywood debut in 2008 in the movie *Speed Racer*. He starred in a couple other Hollywood flicks, including *Ninja Assassin* and *The Prince* while continuing his music and K-drama career in South Korea.

Rainbow

Rainbow is a seven-member girl group that formed in 2009 under DSP Media. The members of Rainbow are Woori, Seungah, Jaekyung, Noeul, Yoonhye, Jisook, and Hyunyoung. In 2009, Rainbow released their music video for the song "Gossip Girl," which was off their *Gossip Girl* EP.

In 2012, a sub-unit group was formed with the members Seungah, Jisook, and Hyunyoung. They were called Rainbow Pixie and they released their first song, "Hoi Hoi," in January 2012. In January 2014, a second sub-unit group was formed called Rainbow Blaxx. It included members Jaekyung, Woori, Seungah, and Hyunyoung.

It was confirmed in October of 2016 that once the members' contracts ended, the members would not re-sign with the agency. Rainbow disbanded in November of 2016.

Rainz

Rainz is a boy group of seven members who were all a part of the second season of the reality survivor show *Produce 101*. Due to high demand from their fan base, this group was formed. The members include Kim Seong-Ri, Ju Won-Tak, Lee Ki-Won, Jang Dae-Hyeon, Hong Eun-Ki, Byun Hyun-Min, and Seo Sung-Hyuk. They released their first EP in October of 2017, *Sunshine*.

Red Velvet

Red Velvet is an SM Entertainment girl group who debuted in August of 2014. The original members were Irene, Seulgi, Wendy and Joy. They debuted with the single "Happiness." In March of 2015, Yeri was added to the group.

It didn't take long for Red Velvet to become successful. They released their first EP, "Ice Cream Cake," in 2015 and full-length album, *The Red*, that same year; both of which were very well-received by the public. Red Velvet has won many respected awards, some of which include the Golden Disk New Artist Award, Seoul Music Award, Korean Entertainment Arts Award, Melon Music Award, and the Mnet Asian Music Award.

R.ef

R.ef is a K-pop group who debuted in 1995. Their name is an acronym for "rave effect." The trio includes members Lee Sung Wook, Park Chul Woo, and Sung Dae Hyun. They released their first album, *Rave Effect*, in 1995. The released several more albums between 1996 and 1999, but then they went on a break, returning with a song in 2004 titled "Love Is Hard."

Repackaged Album

Repackaged albums are common amongst K-pop groups and artists. They are a re-release of a previous album, but with a couple new songs on it. They can also contain remixes, instrumental versions, or acoustic versions of the songs.

Rhythm Power

Rhythm Power is a hip-hop group who are signed with Amoeba Culture. The members include Hangzoo, Boi B, and Gaegooin. The group is well-known for their participation in the popular rap competition show *Show Me the Money*. In 2015, Gaegooin reached the top 10; in 2016, Boi B reached the top 10; and in 2017, Hangzoo won first place.

Rival

Rival is the term used between two K-pop groups who are competing. It can be because they are from different agencies or because they debuted at similar times or have similar looks, feels, or genre of music. A classic example of two groups who were rivals was H.O.T and Sechskies in the '90s.

Rocoberry

Rocoberry is a duo who is known for producing and composing songs, especially for K-dramas. Roco is a female and Conan is male. They have made songs for dramas like *Goblin*, *Descendants of the Sun*, and *Moon Lovers: Scarlet Heart Ryeo*. The two announced that they will be getting married to each other in September of 2018.

ROMEO

ROMEO is a seven-member K-pop boy group who signed under Pony Canyon Korea and CT Entertainment in 2015. The members are Seunghwan, Yunsung, Milo, Minsung, Kyle, Hyunkyung, and Kangmin. They released a mini-album titled *The Romeo* in May of 2015.

Roo'ra

Roo'ra was originally a four member co-ed K-pop group who debuted in 1994 with their album, *Roots of Reggae*. The original members were Lee Sang-Min, Go Young-Wook, Kim Ji-Hyun, and Shin Jung Hwan. Chae Ri-Na replaced Shin Jung-Hwan in 1995 and Michael Romeo replaced Kim Ji-Hyun in 1996. The group disbanded in 1997, but they reunited in 1999. The group was popular and well-known for their reggae-dance genre.

Rookie

Rookie is the term to describe a new K-pop group or artist who just recently debuted.

The Rose

The Rose is a band who signed under J&Star in 2017. The members of the group are Woosung, Dojoon, Hajoon, and Jaehyeong. They debuted on August 3, 2017 with the single "Sorry," which was a big success. Their second single, "Like We Used To," was released on October 31. Their first mini-album, *Void*, was released on April 16, 2018.

Royal Pirates

Royal Pirates, which was formerly known as Fading from Dawn, debuted in 2004. The original members of the group were Kim

Moon-Chul, Soo-Yoon, and Richard Kim. In April 2008, tragedy struck the group as Richard Kim passed away after getting into a car accident. It was after this tragedy that the band changed their group name to Royal Pirates. James Lee joined Royal Pirates in September of 2009. The group made their debut on the music program Inkigayo on August 25, 2013, where they promoted their single, "Shout Out." Their first Korean EP, *Drawing the Line*, was released on January 15, 2014. On January 31, 2017, James Lee announced his departure from Royal Pirates due to an accident that prevented him from playing the bass guitar.

Running Man

A popular variety show in South Korea which includes cast members Yoo Jae-Suk, Kim Jong-Kook, Haha, Song Ji-Hyo, Lee Kwang-Soo, and Ji Suk-Jin. Gary Kang and Song Joong-Ki were previously part of the cast, but departed from the show. Jeon So-Min and Yang Se-Chan joined the show in 2017.

A lot of K-pop idols and groups make their variety show debuts on this program. Idols have mentioned their love for this show and its quirky games.

Ryan Jhun

Ryan Jhun was born on February 28, 1979. He is well-known in the South Korean music industry for his contributions as a successful producer. He is the founder of the label, Marcan Entertainment. Some of the impressive songs he has produced are SHINee's "Lucifer," Super Junior's "My Love, My Kiss, My Heart," TVXQ's "B.U.T," Red Velvet's "Dumb Dumb," and I.O.I's "Whatta Man."

Sa-cha-won

Sa-cha-won is a slang term used to describe someone who is a little quirky. There are a lot of K-pop idols and celebrities who exhibit some characteristics, especially when they are on variety shows, that display their more endearing and weird side. They call these people "sa-cha-won."

E.g., "Wow, I didn't know Loco had such a different way of thinking. He's so unique and quirky, such a sa-cha-won!"

Sam Kim

Sam Kim is a Korean American K-pop artist who made his first appearance on the singing survivor show *K-Pop Star*. He finished second place in the third season and was able to sign under Antenna Music after his appearance. He released the first part of his EP titled *My Name Is Sam* in March of 2016 and the full-length EP was released in April.

Samuel

Born on January 17, 2002, Samuel was originally part of a hip-hop duo called 1Punch with ONE. The duo was short-lived as they debuted in 2015 and disbanded not too long after.

Samuel became famous when he appeared as a participant on the survivor singing show *Produce 101*. He had gained a huge fan base while being on the show and although he was very popular, he did not make it to the final eleven. Despite not making it to the final group, he started a solo career and was able to release his first EP, *Sixteen*, in August of 2017.

Samuel Seo

Samuel Seo, whose Korean name is Seo Dong-Hyeon, was born on May 3, 1991. He auditioned for Bigdeal Squads collective and signed with them in 2008. His first single was released in 2010, "Raindrop." He released a mixtape, *Now or Never*, in 2011 before enlisting into the military.

In 2013, Samuel released his EP, *Welcome to My Zone*. His first studio album, *Frameworks*, was released on October 2, 2015. He had produced and written all of the songs on the album, which seemed to have paid off as he won the Best R&B & Soul Album at the 13th Korean Music Awards.

San E

San E, whose real name is Jung San, was born on January 23, 1985. San E was born in South Korea, but moved to Atlanta, Georgia when he was in middle school. San E released his first two mixtapes as a rapper in 2008 and 2009: *Ready to Be Signed* and *Ready to Be Famous*. In 2010, he won the award for Best Hip-Hop Song at the 2010 Korean Music Awards. Shortly after, he signed with JYP Entertainment and released his first mini-album, *Everybody Ready?*

In April of 2013, San E left JYP Entertainment and signed under Brand New Music. While under Brand New Music, San E released several singles that topped the charts, and released two more EPs and a full studio album. San E was also no stranger to variety shows, as he's hosted and appeared on *Show Me the Money* 3 and 4, *Unpretty Rapstar* season 1 and 2, and *The Unit*.

Sang-namja

The term that refers to a male who is tough as nails and very manly.
E.g., "Did you see how tough and strong Jota was on that *Law of the Jungle* show? He's such a sang-namja!"

Saranghae

"Sa-rang" means "love" in Korean and "sa-rang-hae" means "I love you." It's a common word that fans like to use on their favorite K-pop groups and idols.

Sasaeng/Sasaeng fan

This is the term that refers to a die-hard fan who is too obsessive. The term "sasaeng fan" is not considered a good thing. Sasaeng fans have stalker-like tendencies and tend to cross the line when it comes to adoring their favorite K-pop groups and celebrities. In extreme cases, they break into the celebrity's house.

Say A

Say A is the name of the fandom for the girl group Miss A.

SBS Gayo Daejeon

At the end of the year in December, SBS hosts a music program. They have had various themes, different every year. For example, in 2017, the theme was to feature all the artists who achieved number one on the charts that year.

Sechskies

Sechskies was originally a six-member boy band who debuted in 1997. They are one of the first K-pop idol groups that were formed. The original members were Eun Ji-Won, Lee Jae-Jin, Kim Jae-Duk, Kang Sung-Hoon, Go Ji-Yong and Jang Su-Won.

Secshkies debuted with the song "School Anthem," which was also the name of the first album they released. Although it became a hit song, the song that really put them on the map was "Pomseng-pomsa." The success of their first album put them in competition with H.O.T, who were the number one boy group at the time. There were two fandoms to choose from—team Sechskies or team H.O.T.

Despite their success, Sechskies disbanded in May of 2000, just three years after their debut. Their fans were devastated, to say the least. However, sixteen years later, the group was able to reunite through the hit variety show *Infinite Challenge* and were able to perform a concert for their fans. Go Ji-Yong was the only member who did not partake in this reunion. Shortly after their appearance on *Infinite Challenge*, the group signed with YG Entertainment.

Secret

Secret is a K-pop girl group who debuted under TS Entertainment in 2009. The members include Jung Ha-Na, Han Sun-Hwa, Song Ji-Eun, and Jun Hyo-Seong. The first single they released was called "I Want You Back." The following year, they released two more singles, "Magic" and "Madonna," that gained quite a bit of attention. That same year, they won the Newcomer Award at the 25th Golden Disc Awards

In 2016, Sunhwa left the group and the remaining three members wanted to continue with the group, but were unable to do so due to some issues with their agency. The group had no choice but to disband.

Selca

The Korean word used to refer to "selfies." Koreans love taking selcas and uploading them onto their social media accounts.

Seo In-Guk

Seo In-Guk was born on October 23, 1987. He gained fame after appearing in the first season of the reality singing elimination program *Superstar K*. He won first place, impressing the public with his smooth and killer vocals.

Seo In-Guk made his acting debut in the K-drama *Love Rain*. Although the role was a smaller one, it was able to kick-start his acting career. He later landed the starring role in the hit series *Reply 1997*. His debut as a male lead was a huge success as people were impressed with his acting. He also sang two songs on the soundtrack, which became big hits. In 2014, he released his first studio album, *Everlasting*.

Seo Taiji

Seo Taiji, otherwise known as Jung Hyun-Chul, was born on February 21, 1972. He is a musician, singer, songwriter, and producer who was originally part of a heavy metal group called Sinawe. In 1992, he formed Seo Taiji and Boys, which is what he is known for today. The group promoted together for four years and gained a lot of success in Korea, garnering a huge following. After disbanding Seo Taiji and Boys, he continued a solo career as a singer, experimenting with various genres of music. Every album he released had a different feel and sound.

In Seo Taiji's solo career, he was nominated for and won several awards, including the Mnet Asian Music Award for Best Rock Performance (2002), Best Rock Video (2004), and Best Male Artist (2008).

Seo Taiji and Boys

Seo Taiji and Boys are considered to be the pioneers of K-pop music. The group debuted in April 1992 and disbanded in 1996. Members included Seo Taiji, Yang Hyun-Suk, and Lee Juno. They introduced various genres of music, especially hip-hop, to the public and were really the ones to pave the way in the South Korean music industry for other K-pop artists and groups.

The group debuted with the song "Nan Arayo" ("I Know"). It was a type of music that South Korea was not used to hearing, but it still became successful. They released a music video for the song, and their first album sold over 1.5 million copies within a month. In 1996, despite their success and ever-growing popularity, Seo Taiji and Boys decided to disband. It was a huge disappointment to millions of fans as it was a decision that was made quite suddenly.

In addition to the huge impact that the trio made in the Korean music industry, they also won several awards including the Golden Disc Award for Best Artist for three years in a row (1992 to 1994), the Popularity Award in 1995, the Grand Prize at the Seoul Music Awards in 1992 and 1993, and the Main Prize in 1993 and 1995.

Seol-nal

A holiday in South Korea that celebrates the lunar new year. It is considered to be one of the bigger holidays in South Korea. A lot of K-pop artists and celebrities wear hanboks or like to convey their best wishes and blessings for the new year on this special day.

Seoul Music Awards

Seoul Music Awards brings recognition to those artists who have released albums that year. The winners are based on mobile votes, digital downloads, album sales, and judges' scores. The categories for the Seoul Music Awards are as follows: Daesang Award (Grand Prize), Bonsang Award (Main Prize), Record of the Year, Record of the Year in Digital Release, New Artist Award, Performance Award, Trot Award, Hip-Hop Award, R&B/Ballad Award, OST Award, Popularity Award, and Hallyu Special Award.

Seoul Olympic Stadium

The Seoul Olympic Stadium was originally built for the 1988 Summer Olympics, and is now used for various events and concerts including those of many K-pop groups. It's an impressive venue to hold a concert as it can hold up to 69,950 people. Some of the K-pop groups who have performed at this venue include H.O.T, JYJ, g.o.d, EXO, and BTS.

Seoul World Cup Stadium

The Seoul World Cup Stadium is mainly a venue used for soccer events, originally built to accomodate the 2002 FIFA World Cup. It is the second largest stadium in South Korea (the first being The Seoul Olympic Stadium), and it has 66,704 seats. Many K-pop groups and idols hold their concerts here, including PSY, Sechskies, BIGBANG, G-Dragon, and several Dream Concerts.

S.E.S

S.E.S is a veteran girl group who signed under SM Entertainment in 1997. The members of S.E.S were Bada, Eugene, and Shoo; their names also make up the acronym of their group name (Bada means "sea" in Korean). The trio released their album, *I'm Your Girl*, which was very well-received by the public. They became the girl group to challenge and compete against when it came to the specific time and era. Their success and momentum didn't stop there. They released their second album, *Sea & Eugene & Shoo*, with the hit song "Dreams Come True" and their third album in 1999, *Love*, which was their bestselling album. Their fourth album was released in 2000, *A Letter From Greenland*; their fifth album, *Choose My Life-U*, in 2002; and sixth album, *Remember*, in 2017.

When it came to awards, S.E.S dominated, especially during their first few years as K-pop stars. They won the Golden Disk Award for New Artist of the Year in 1998, Bonsang Award in 1999, and Popularity Award in 2001. They also won the Bonsang in 1998 at the Seoul Music Awards and the Best Female Group Award for Best Female Group in 2001 and 2002 at the Mnet Asian Music Awards.

Sadly, in December of 2002, the trio officially disbanded. However, much to their fans' delight, they returned to celebrate their 20th anniversary in 2016. Following this return, they released their 20th anniversary special, titled "Remember," in January 2017.

Se7en

Se7en (pronounced "seven") was born on November 9, 1984. He signed under YG Entertainment as a trainee in 1999, but did not debut until 2003. He released his first song, "Come Back To Me," and then released his album, *Just Listen*. Due to his huge success in Korea, plans were made for Se7en to debut in the US. His first US single, "Girls," was released in March of 2008.

Se7en made his return to Korea on July of 2010 with the mini-album *Digital Bounce*. He released his second mini-album in February of 2012 in Japan with the song "When I Can't Sing." In March of 2013, Se7en enlisted into the army; after he completed his services, his contract with YG Entertainment expired and the two parties decided not to renew the contract. He released the track "I'm Good" after leaving YG and also released a mini-album titled *I Am Se7en*.

Throughout Se7en's singing career, he released four albums in Korea, one album in China, and three albums in Japan. He also received quite a lot of awards, some of which include the Bonsang Award (Main Award) at the Golden Disk Awards, KBS Music Awards, and the MBC Music Awards in 2004. He also won several Best New Artist/Singer Awards in 2003 when he first debuted.

Seventeen

Seventeen is a boy band that has thirteen members and three sub-units. The members of the group are as follows: S.Coups, Jeonghan, Joshua, Jun, Hoshi, Wonwoo, Woozi, DK, Mingyu, The8, Seungkwan, Vernon, and Dino. Seventeen signed under Pledis Entertainment in 2015 and debuted on May 26. Their first EP, *17 Carat*, was released just a few nights after their debut. The album was well received, especially in the US, and it became the longest-charting K-pop album of the year. In September, the boys released their second EP, *Boys Be*, which also became a huge success.

Seventeen is divided into three sub-unit groups. The Hip-Hop Unit has members S.Coups, Wonwoo, Mingyu, and Vernon. The Vocal Unit members are Jeonghan, Joshua, Woozi, DK, and Seungkwan. And the Performance Unit is Jun, Hoshi, The8, and Dino.

Although the group is fairly new, they have been nominated for and won many awards. Some of these awards include the Golden Disk Award for Rookie of the year in 2016, Disc Bonsang in 2017 and 2018, Mnet Asian Music Awards for Best World Performer in 2016, Worldwide Favorite Artist in 2017, and Best Dance Performance—Male Group in 2017 and Seoul Music Awards for New Artist in 2016, Bonsang Award in 2017 and 2018.

SF9

SF9, which stands for "Sensational Feeling 9," is a boy band signed under FNC Entertainment. The members of SF9 are Youngbin, Inseong, Jaeyoon, Dawon, Rowoon, Zuho, Taeyang, Hwiyoung, and Chani. They debuted in October of 2016, releasing their first album, *Feeling Sensation*.

With the success of their debut, SF9 was able to snag Best Rookie of the Year Awards for the Seoul Success Awards and Fandom School Awards in 2017.

SG Wannabe

SG Wannabe has a unique group name as it stands for "Simon and Garfunkel" (the famous American folk rock duo). They debuted in 2004 with the album *SG Wanna Be+*, and their first music video featured a lot of famous actors at the time, which made the trio rise to popularity fairly quickly. On top of the music video, people were drawn to their amazing vocals and were impressed with the quality and sound of their music. Their popularity was recognized when they won the SBS Gayo Daejun Award for Best Newcomer, 19th Golden Disk Award for Best Newcomer, and the Seoul Music Award for Best Newcomer, all in that same year.

S#arp

S#arp (pronounced "Sharp") was a very successful co-ed K-pop group who debuted in the late '90s. The original members were Lee Ji-Hye, Seo Ji-Young, Jang Seok-Hyun, John Kim, and Oh Hee-Jong, but John Kim and Oh Hee Jong left the group after the release of their first album, *The S#arp*. Jeon Ji-Young (Sori) and Chris Kim joined the group and stayed until it disbanded.

Shawols

Shawols is the name for fans of SHINee. The word "shawol" is a shortened version of "SHINee" and "world."

SHINee

SHINee is a boy group which was formed in 2008 under SM Entertainment. The original members of SHINee included the leader Onew, Key, Minho, Taemin, and Jonghyun. Unfortunately, in December of 2017, Jonghyun passed away and the remaining four members have honored Jonghyun by continuing their careers as a four member group.

SHINee first debuted in 2008 with their EP, *Replay*, in which they released their hit single, "Noona Neomu Yeppeo" (translation: "Noona, You're so Pretty"). In 2008, they released their album titled *The SHINee World*. Following this album, they released five more studio albums, all of which were huge hits. Some famous songs that the group is known for are "Ring Ding Dong" (2008), "Lucifer" (2010), "Sherlock" (2012), "Dream Girl" (2013), "Everybody" (2013), "View" (2015) and many more.

SHINee's success is also shown in the immense amount of awards that they have won. Pretty much any time they are nominated, they are sure to win. Some of the impressive awards they have won are the Disc Bonsang Award at the Golden Disc Awards in 2010, 2013, 2014, 2016, and 2017. They also won the Popularity Award in 2009, 2010, 2013, 2014, 2016, and 2017. They won the Bonsang Award at the Seoul Music Awards in 2010, 2011, 2013, 2014, 2016, and 2017. And the Best Dance Performance—Male Group at the Mnet Asian Music Awards in 2012, 2013, and 2015.

As a result of the popularity of SHINee, the group has done three tours across Asia and two tours in various parts all around the world. Their success has also crossed into Japan as they did Japanese tours almost every year from 2012 to 2018.

Shinhwa

Shinhwa is a six-member boy group who signed under SM Entertainment in 1998. Their name means "legend" in Korean. The members of the group are Eric Mun, Lee Min-Woo, Kim Dong-Wan, Shin Hye-Sung, Jun Jin, and Andy Lee. The group has stayed together since their debut, which is very impressive in the K-pop world. They are considered to be one of the oldest K-pop groups in the industry.

Shinhwa made their first TV appearance in March of 1998 with their song, "Resolver." Although their songs were good, they were not well-received by the public as their rival group, H.O.T, was far too strong in popularity. Despite the negative response, Shinhwa released their second album, *T.O.P*, in April of 1999. The public started to warm up to them and they even won the Best Male Group Award that same year at the Mnet Asian Music Awards.

In 2003, Shinhwa's contract with SM Entertainment came to an end. The group decided to take a bit of a break in 2008 as many of them went to fulfill their mandatory military service. In 2011, the group made their own company, Shinhwa Company, and they released their tenth album together, *The Return*.

Shinsadong Tiger

Shinsadong Tiger, whose real name is Lee Ho-Yang, was born on June 3, 1983. He is a producer that has produced a lot of famous K-pop tunes that people know today. He has produced mega-hit songs like 4Minute's "Hot Issue," Beast's "Fiction," Apink's

"NoNoNo," and Ailee's "U&I." He has won some prestigious awards, which include the Digital Daesang Award at the Golden Disk Awards (2008), the Bonsang Award at the Seoul Music Awards (2011), and the Song Writer Award at the Melon Music Awards (2013).

Ship/Shipping

The term used when you really love a couple. The couple can be fictitious or a real-life couple. For example, a common situation in which people may "ship" a couple is when they watch a K-drama or a variety show and see two people who have a lot of chemistry with each other.

E.g., "Did you see P.O. and Sandara on that variety show?"

"Yes! How cute are they together?!"

"OMG, I hope they date in real life. I totally ship them!"

Show Champion

Show Champion is a South Korean music show that airs every Wednesday. Various K-pop groups and artists perform on this show.

Show Me the Money

Show Me the Money is a reality rap competition show that has aired on Mnet since 2012. The premise of the show is to have contestants rap in front of a panel of judges and producers. The judges are the ones who eliminate the rappers until the group is smaller, which is when the public is able to vote. The show is known for the rap battles and songs that the producers compose for the rappers. Some popular rappers who have gained popularity as a result of the show are BewhY, Junoflo, Basick, Bobby (of iKON), and Swings.

Show! Music Core

Show! Music Core is a music program that is run by MBC. It airs every Saturday and is a live music program, featuring various K-pop idols, groups and artists. There are first place winners announced weekly based on album/digital sales, music video views, viewer voting, radio broadcasting, and audience live voting.

Sistar

Sistar is a girl group who was signed under the agency Starship Entertainment. The members got together in 2010 and they released their first album, *So Cool*, in August of 2011. The group includes four members: Bora, Hyolyn, Soyou, and Dasom. The group has a very sexy and sensual image that has brought them a lot of success, not to mention their killer vocals and dance moves.

The success of Sistar is evident in the fact that they have also been nominated for a countless number of awards and have won most of the categories they have been nominated for. They have won the Top 10 Bonsang Award at the Melon Music Awards four years in a row (2012–2015) and have won Song of the Year for the Gaon Chart Music Awards in 2013, 2014, and 2016.

Despite the killer success of the group, Sistar revealed that they would be separating in May 2017. They had been together for seven years at that point. Their last performance was in June 2017 on the music program Inkigayo, where they performed their big hits: "Touch My Body," "Shake It," "Loving U," "I Swear," and their latest release, "Lonely."

Sistar19

Sistar19 is a sub-unit of Sistar that debuted in 2011. The members of this sub-unit were Hyolyn and Bora. The first song they released together was titled "Ma Boy" in 2011. In January of 2013, they released an EP titled *Gone Not Around Any Longer*.

Skinship

The term used to describe any sort of physical touch between two people. In the Korean culture, it is a big deal when people make skin to skin contact, no matter how subtle or small the touch is. They refer to this as "skinship."

S-Line

S-Line is the term used to describe a person's figure. If a woman has a curvy body, similar to that of an hourglass, they would say she has an S-Line body. An example of a K-pop idol who has an S-Line body is Hyorin.

SM Entertainment

SM Entertainment is one of the "Big 3" entertainment agencies in South Korea. It was established in 1995 by Lee Soo Man, who used to be a recording artist. The agency started with the signing of the successful boy group H.O.T in 1996, followed by the successful girl group S.E.S in 1997. It is also home to a lot of famous veteran

K-pop groups and artists who paved the way for K-pop groups today like Shinhwa, Fly to the Sky, and BoA.

With the success of these veteran K-pop groups and artists, SM expanded even more and produced K-pop groups who continued to represent SM Entertainment through their success and international recognition. These artists include Girls' Generation, SHINee, and Super Junior. Some more current K-pop groups that are signed under SM are EXO, Red Velvet, f(x), and NCT.

SM Town

SM Town is the name given for all the K-pop idols and groups under SM Entertainment. There is an SM Town Live World Tour every year where the SM Town artists perform, and videos are uploaded onto the SMTOWN YouTube channel with performances by the SM Town artists.

SMTOWN Coex Artium

If you're a fan of SM artists, this is the perfect place to visit. Located in Gangnam, SMTOWN Coex Artium offers six floors of pure SM artist entertainment. There's a merchandise store where you can purchase all kinds of memorabilia or souvenirs including clothing, shoes, pillows, calendars, makeup products, and even snacks. You can also find a cafe in the building with pastries, cakes, and drinks with unique names that pay tribute to various groups and singers. Another cool part about the cafe is that the seats and tables are signed by some SM artists themselves. On the top floors of the building, there is the SMTOWN theatre where you can watch musicals, plays, concerts, and showcases of your favorite SM singers.

SNS

SNS is an abbreviation for "Social Networking Service." It is a term that Koreans use often to refer to social media platforms.

E.g., "I can't believe I got to take a picture with Taeyeon! I'm going to upload it on my SNS."

Snuper

Snuper is a boy band that signed with Widmay Entertainment in 2015. They debuted on November 16, 2015 with their EP titled *Shall We*. The members of the group are Suhyun, Sangil, Taewoong, Woosung, Sangho, and Sebin.

Solbangul

The name that SONAMOO gives their fans. Solbangul in Korean means "pine cone." Their fans are referred to as "pine cones" because their group name means "pine tree" in Korean.

Solid

Solid is a trio who debuted in 1993. The members of the group are Johan Kim, Jaeyoon Chong, and Joon Lee. The members had met in California before going to South Korea in 1993 to start their music career. They released their first album on December 15, 1993, *Give Me a Chance*. It was a struggle for them to get the album recognized, but then the release of their second album, *The*

Magic of 8 Ball, sparked their career. The song "Holding the End of the Night" off the album was a huge success and continues to be a song that is recognized today. On April 1, 1996, the group released their third album, *Light Camera Action!*, and Solid continued on the road of success. Their fourth album was released on April 24, 1997, *Solidate*. This was the last album the trio released until twenty-one years later when they announced a reunion and comeback. *Into the Light* was released on March 22, 2018.

SONAMOO

SONAMOO is a girl group that debuted in December of 2014 under TS Entertainment. The members of the group are Sunmin, Minjae, D.ana, Nahyun, Euijin, High.D, and NewSun. They debuted with the release of their EP, *Deja Vu*. It hit number one of the Gaon's Weekly Album chart, which was considered a great accomplishment. The group released their second EP, *Cushion*, in July of 2015 and their third EP, *I Like U Too Much*, in June of 2016.

In 2017, SONAMOO won the New Korean Wave Music Star Award at the Soribada K-Music Awards

Sone

The name that the girl group Girls' Generation has for their fandom. It is pronounced "sowon."

Soompi

Soompi is the name of a popular website that brings news and features to everything Korean Entertainment. It first started in 1998 by Susan Kang, who was a fan of H.O.T. Since then, it's become a source for providing fans all over the world with content on their favorite K-pop stars and celebrities.

Soribada

Soribada was originally an online file-sharing service that was launched in 2000. The direct translation of Soribada in Korean is "Ocean of Sound." The file sharing platform was relaunched as an MP3 service in December of 2004.

Soribada Best K-Music Awards

In 2017, Soribada hosted the first ever Soribada Best K-Music Awards. The awards are based on Soribada data, mobile votes, and ratings from critics.

Some of the artists who won the first ever Soribada Awards in 2017 were EXO, TWICE, Wanna One, BTS, Red Velvet, and Pentagon.

Special Stage

Special stages are performances that K-pop idols or artists do as a token of appreciation for their fans. Some "special stage" performances can be K-pop groups covering other group's songs or two idols from two different groups coming together to do a dance or sing a song.

Spica

Spica is a girl group who debuted in 2012 under B2M Entertainment. The members are Kim Boa, Park Sihyun, Park Narae, Yang Jiwon, and Kim Bohyung. The released a single prior to their debut titled "Doggedly" in January of 2012 and then released a mini-album titled *Russian Roulette* the following month.

Spica S

A sub-unit of Spica that was formed in September 2014. The members of Spica S were Park Sihyun, Park Narae, Yang Jiwon, and Kim Bohyung. They released the song "Give Your Love" in September of 2014.

SS501

SS501 signed with DSP Entertainment in 2005 and debuted their EP, *Warning*, that same year. The members of the group are Kim Hyun-Joong, Heo Young-Saeng, Kim Kyu-Jong, Park Jung-Min, and Kim Hyung-Jun. The group became an instant success as they won Best New Male Group at the Mnet KM Music Festival, and Best New Artist at the 2005 SBS Gayo Awards as well as the MBC Music Festival. In 2006, they released their first full album, *S.T 01 Now*. That year they won the Bonsang at the SBS Gayo Awards, and the Disc Bonsang at the 21st Golden Disc Awards

Stan

The term used when you are a hardcore fan of a K-pop group or K-pop idol.

E.g., "I stan Wanna One" or "I'm a BTS stan."

Starship Entertainment

Starship Entertainment is an entertainment agency that was founded by Kim Shi Dae in 2008. Kim Shi Dae used to be the manager for the K-pop group Cool before starting his own company. Some K-pop idols that had signed under Starship are K.Will, MONSTA X, Boyfriend, Cosmic Girls, and Sistar.

Stellar

Stellar is a girl group who was formed in 2011 under The Entertainment Pascal. The original members of the group were Leeseul, JoA, Gayoung, and Jeonyul. The first single they released was "Rocket Girl" in August of 2011, but it was not very successful. After their debut, Lee Seul and JoA left the group and Minhee and Hyoeun became the new members. In May of 2017, Soyoung joined the group and in August of 2017, Youngheun joined as well.

In February of 2018, Hyoeun and Minhee did not renew their contracts with the agency, which meant the group would be disbanding.

Stray Kids

Stray Kids is a boy band that was formed under JYP Entertainment. They had a reality show titled *Stray Kids* that brought them a lot of popularity prior to their debut. The members of the group are Woojin, Bang Chan, Lee Know, Changbin, Hyunjin, Han, Felix, Seungmin, and I.N.

Stray Kids released a pre-debut EP titled *Mixtape* in January 2018 that was a success. Their official debut came in March 2018 with the EP *I Am Not*.

Sub-unit

Sub-unit is the term used for when a K-pop group is formed within a larger group.

E.g., GD & Taeyang are a sub-unit group of BIGBANG, JJ Project (Jinyoung and JB) are a sub-unit group of GOT7.

Sunbae

Sunbae is a term used towards someone who has been working in the same field as you for a longer period of time. It's a term of respect that acknowledges hierarchy in an industry and is taken very seriously in Korean culture. In the K-pop entertainment world, it is necessary for fellow K-pop stars to refer to other artists and groups who have debuted even a day earlier than them as sunbae.

Sunny Hill

Sunny Hill debuted in September of 2007 under For Everyone Media. It was originally a co-ed group with members Janghyun, Jubi, and Seung Ah. They released their single album, *Love Letter*, followed by their second single album, *2008 My Summer*.

In 2010, Sunny Hill changed agencies to Nega Network and announced that there would be a new member, Kota, in the group and later, Misung. Sunny Hill made another agency change and switched to LOEN Entertainment where they released an EP titled *Midnight Circus*. In January of 2012, Janghyun enlisted into the military and on April 14, Sunny Hill made a comeback as a girl group.

Super Junior

Super Junior is a boy group that was formed under SM Entertainment. The original members of the group were Leeteuk, Heechul, Hangeng, Yesung, Kangin, Shindong, Sungmin, Eunhyuk, Donghae, Siwon, Ryeowook, and Kibum. Kyuhyun joined in 2006.

Super Junior made their official debut on the music program *Popular Song* in November of 2005. They performed their singles "Twins (Knock Out)" and "You Are the One." Their first album, *Twins*, was released in December of 2005. In May of 2006, the group released a free single titled "U" that gained a lot of success. Super Junior won several awards at the end of the year. Their third album, *Sorry, Sorry*, was released on March of 2009 and topped charts in South Korea.

Super Junior has continued to gain success and have in total completed three Asian tours and four world tours. They've also been nominated for 216 awards and won 161 of them, which is an impressive feat.

Super Junior-D&E

Super Junior-D&E is a sub-unit group of Super Junior that debuted in December of 2011 with the song "Oppa Oppa." The "D&E" in the name stands for the two members who are in the group, which are Donghae and Eunhyuk. The duo embarked on their first Japan Tour in 2014 and gained a lot of attention in Japan, even winning the Popularity Award at the Asia Model Awards in 2015. They also won the Album of the Year and Best 3 Album Award at the Japan Gold Disc Awards in 2015.

Super Junior-H

Super Junior-H, in which the "H" stands for "Happy," is another sub-unit group of Super Junior that was formed in 2008. The members of Super Junior-H are Leeteuk, Yesung, Kangin, Shindong, Sungmin, and Eunhyuk. The group released their first EP, *Cooking? Cooking!*, and music video on June of 2008. After their EP and music video release, the group performed their single at the 2008 Dream Concert and also had a fan meeting. They released their second single, "Pajama Party," in August of 2008.

Super Junior-K.R.Y

Super Junior-K.R.Y is a sub-unit that was formed in 2006. The members of this sub-unit were Kyuhyun, Ryeowook, and Yesung. Their first single was titled "The One I Love." The group did a concert tour of Asia in 2010–2011 and held a special concert in 2012.

Super Junior-M

Super Junior-M, also known as SJ-M, is a sub-unit group of Super Junior. The "M" in the name stands for "Mandarin." It was formed specifically to target the Chinese music industry and included members that were both Chinese and Korean. The original members of this group were Han Geng, Donghae, Siwon, Ryeowook, Kyuhyun, Zhou Mi, and Henry. Han Geng departed from the group in 2009 and Henry left the group in 2018. They later added Super Junior members Eunhyuk and Sungmin to the group.

Super Junior-M debuted in Beijing in April of 2008. They released the music video for their song, "U," which was originally a Super Junior song. Their debut album titled *Me* was released in April of 2008.

The success of Super Junior-M was shown in the plethora of awards that they were nominated for and won. Some of these awards included winning Most Popular Group at the Southeast Explosive Music Chart Awards (2008), Asia's Most Popular New Group at the Music King Awards (2008), Most Popular Group of the Year Award at the Global Chinese Golden Chart Awards (2011), Favorite Musical Band and Group at the 14th Top Chinese Award (2014), and many more.

Super Junior-T

Super Junior-T is a sub-unit group of Super Junior that was formed in 2007. Members included Leeteuk, Heechul, Kangin, Sungmin, Shindong, and Eunhyuk. This group was specifically focused on the trot genre. They released their first single, "Rokuko," in February of 2007.

Supernova

Supernova is a boy group that signed under Mnet Media in 2006. The members of the group include Jung Yun-Hak, Kim Sung-Je, Kim Kwang-Su, Yoon Sung-Mo, Song Ji-Hyuk, and Park Geon-Il. They debuted with the song "HIT" on *Music Bank* in September of 2007 and released their first album, *The Beautiful Stardust*, shortly after. *The Beautiful Stardust* was the only Korean album that was released as Supernova continued to release seven more Japanese albums between 2009 and 2015. In June of 2018, it was announced that Supernova had ended their contracts with their agency.

Superstar K

A South Korean television show that is a reality singing program. Contestants audition for the program and have to get through to several rounds until they are in the final one. The winner wins various prizes as well as a chance to perform at the Mnet Asian Music Awards. The winners of the seasons are as follows: Seo In-Guk (2009), Huh Gak (2010), Ulala Session (2011), Roy Kim (2012), Parc Jae-Jung (2013), Kwak Jin-Eon (2014), Kevin Oh (2015), and Kim Young Geun (2016).

Swings

Swings, whose real name is Moon Ji-Hoon, was born on October 14, 1986. He is a rapper who debuted in 2008 with the release of his EP, *Upgrade*. His first full album, *Growing Pains*, was released in 2010. Despite the release of these albums, Swings' rise to fame came after being a contestant on the second season of the rap competition show *Show Me the Money*. The following year, he returned on the show as a producer alongside San E and Tablo.

In August of 2014, Swings left his label Brand New Music and started his own label, Just Music Entertainment.

Tablo

Tablo, whose real name is Lee Seon-Woong (Daniel Lee), is a rapper, producer, and writer. He is the leader of the hip-hop trio Epik High and also founded the indie music label HIGHGRND.

Tablo graduated from Stanford University and then moved to Korea where he formed Epik High. In 2008, Tablo became an author as he published his book, *Pieces of You*. It became a best-seller in Korea. In September of 2011, Tablo signed with YG Entertainment and released the song "Airbag" the following month. He released the first part of his EP titled *Fever's End* in October of 2011 and then part two in November.

TaeTiSeo

TaeTiSeo (TTS) is a sub-unit of Girls' Generation. The members include Taeyeon, Tiffany, and Seohyun. On April 29, 2012, they debuted with their EP, *Twinkle*, which became an instant success as they reached triple crown status on the music shows. Their success didn't stop with their second EP, *Holler*, which was released in September of 2014. They even had their own reality series, *The*

TaeTiSeo, that gave an insight into the members' everyday lives. In December of 2015, the trio released their third EP, *Dear Santa*, and a portion of their sales went to the charity organization SMile for U.

T-ara

T-ara is a girl group who was was formed under MBK Entertainment in 2009. Their name is a shortened version of the word "tiara" which would represent the fact that they are "queens of the music industry." The original members of the group were Jiae, Jiwon, Eunjung, Hyomin, and Jiyeon. They released their first song, "Joheun Saram," which means "good person" in Korean. In June of 2009, Jiae and Jiwon left T-ara and Boram, Soyeon, and Qri were added.

T-ara debuted on the talk show *Radio Star* in July of 2009 and made their stage debut on the music show *M Countdown* later in July. They released their first studio album, *Absolute First Album*, in November of 2009. They won the Rookie of the Year Award that year at the 24th Golden Disc Awards In July of 2010, Hwayoung was added to T-ara, but her career was short-lived as her contract was terminated in July of 2012. Shortly after Hwayoung left the group, Areum was added to the group.

Soyeon and Boram did not renew their contracts when they ended in May of 2017. Qri, Eunjung, Hyomin, and Jiyeon stayed with the agency until the end of the year. In January of 2018, Hyomin, Jiyeon, Eunjung, and Qri decided to leave the company.

T-ara N4

T-ara N4 is a sub-unit group of T-ara that was formed in March 2013. The original members were Eunjung, Hyomin, Jiyeon, and

Areum, but Areum left the group in July of 2013. They debuted in April of 2013, releasing the single "Jeon Won Diary."

Teaser

The K-pop world is all about the teasers. A lot of agencies release teaser images or clips of music videos that hint at the release of an album or song.

Teddy

Teddy, whose Korean name is Park Hong-Jun, was born on September 14, 1978. In 1998, Teddy debuted in the YG Entertainment hip-hop group 1TYM. After 1TYM disbanded in 2005, Teddy continued to work under YG as a producer. He is considered to be one of the most successful producers in the K-pop industry, having produced songs for big names like 2NE1, BIGBANG, BLACKPINK, and other YG artists.

Teen Top

Teen Top is a boy group that was formed in 2010 under TOP Media. The group originally consisted of six members: C.A.P, Chunji, Nile, Ricky, Changjo, and L.Joe. In July of 2010, Teen Top made their debut with the song "Clap," which was off their single album, *Come Into the World*. The group released two studio albums titled *No. 1* (2013) and *High Five* (2017). L.Joe left the group right before the release of their second studio album, making Teen Top a five-member group.

10cm

10cm is a band that consists of members Kwon Jung-Yeol and Yoon Cheol-Jong. They debuted in 2010 with their EP titled *The First EP*. They were well-received and even won the Discovery of the Year Award at the Mnet Asian Music Awards that same year. Their second EP, *The 2nd EP*, was released on February 4, 2013. The group disbanded in 2017 as Yoon Cheol-Jong left the group.

Title Track

Title track refers to the song that the group or idol promotes that also happens to have the same title as their album.

Topp Dogg

A boy group with Stardom Entertainment that debuted in 2013. Topp Dogg originally had thirteen members, but currently has five. The original thirteen were Hojoon, Sangdo, B-Joo, Xero, Sangwon, Seogoong, Gohn, Kidoh, Jenissi, P-Goon, Nakta, Hansol, and A-Tom. Topp Dogg debuted by having a showcase in October of 2013. They also released their music video for "Follow Me" and released their EP, *Dogg's Out*, the day after.

In July of 2015, Topp Dogg was moved to Hunus Entertainment as their former agency had merged with Hunus. In February of 2018, the group changed their name to Xeno-T, which is a combination of the words "xenogeneic" and "top-class." The current members of Topp Dogg are Hojoon, Sangdo, B-Joo, Xero, and Sangwon.

ToppKlass

The name Topp Dogg gives their fans.

Toronto Kpop Con

Toronto Kpop Con is a music festival that happens annually over the span of three days. Based in Toronto, it features several K-pop groups throughout the event as well as fanmeets, YouTuber panels, workshops, and other well-known performers showcasing their skills. Some past K-pop groups at the conference include VIXX, GFriend, GOT7, DAY6, K.A.R.D, and BtoB.

Trainee

It is well-known in the K-pop industry that most K-pop idols go through a long and strenuous training program before debuting. This can take anywhere from months to years and their days are usually spent practicing dancing, singing, rapping, and partaking in other K-pop-related activities.

Trash

Trash is the term a lot of K-pop fans use to say that they are a huge fan of a group.

E.g., Friend 1: "I'm in love with BTS. I watched all their interviews last night!"

Friend 2: "Ditto. I'm so BTS trash."

TraxX

TraxX, also known as Trax or The TRAX, is a rock group that was formed under SM Entertainment. The original members of the group were Typhoon Jay, Rose Minwoo, Attack Jungwoo, and Xmas Jungmo. Their group name was an acronym for their first names. The group released their debut single titled "Paradox" in July of 2004. Their second single was titled "Scorpio" and it was released in Japan in November of 2004. In 2006 and 2007, Minwoo and Jungwoo left the group, leaving the group as a duo with members Jay and Jungmo.

Trax released their mini-album, *Cold-Hearted Man*, in January of 2010; their second mini-album, *Oh! My Goddess*, in September of 2010; and their third mini-album, *Blind*, in November of 2011. Jay and Jungmo enlisted into the military for their mandatory service shortly after and the group went on a hiatus.

In July of 2015, Trax performed again at the SM Town Live Tour IV. It was announced in March of 2018 that Trax would change their name to TraxX and that GINJO would join the group.

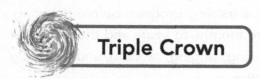

Triple Crown

The Triple Crown is a big achievement for a K-pop group or artists. A K-pop group is awarded the "Triple Crown" title when their song reaches number one on the three major Korean music shows, which are *M Countdown*, *Music Bank*, and *Inkigayo*.

Triple H

Triple H is a co-ed group that was formed by Cube Entertainment. The group consists of Hyuna, Hui, and E'Dawn. Hui and E'Dawn are members of the group Pentagon, who are also signed under the same agency. On May 1, 2017, the group released an EP titled *199X* with the single and music video for the song "365 Fresh."

Trot

Trot is a genre in Korean pop music that originated sometime between 1910 and 1945. The term "trot" came from "foxtrot," which is a type of dance that has two-beat rhythms. After World War II, trot music became more popular and Koreans started to bring in Western influences to Korean music. By the time the 1980s came and other genres of music were introduced to the Korean culture, trot music began to lose some of its appeal.

Trouble Maker

Trouble Maker is a sub-unit group that was formed by Cube Entertainment. This duo is made up of members Hyun-Seung and Hyuna. On December 1, 2011, they released an EP titled *Trouble Maker*. The response for this duo was good as they won several awards that following year including the Best Dance Performance at the 27th Golden Disk Awards, Hot Trend Song at the 4th Melon Music Awards, and the Best Collaboration Performance at the 14th Mnet Asian Music Awards. On October 28, 2013, they released their second EP, *Chemistry*, with the single "Now (There is No Tomorrow)."

Turbo

Turbo is a K-pop duo who debuted in 1995. The original members were Kim Jong-Kook and Kim Jung-Nam. They released their first album in 1995, *280 km/h Speed*. With the songs "My Childhood Dream," "Black Cat," and "Choices," Turbo was quickly becoming a popular K-pop dance duo. Their second album was released in 1996, *New Sensation*. Their song, "Twist King," was a huge success. Shortly after the release of their second album, Kim Jung-Nam left the group and was replaced by Mikey.

In October of 1997, Turbo returned with their third album, *Born Again*. Their songs "December" and "Goodbye Yesterday" were instant successes. However, after the release of their fourth album, *Perfect Love*, Turbo was banned from appearing on shows due to Kim Jong-Kook's rude behavior at a concert. Once they were given permission to appear on TV again, the duo returned with their fifth album, *Email My Heart*. Just like the other albums released previously, it was a big success. Shortly after the fifth album, however, Kim Jong-Kook left the agency and Mikey returned to the US. Although Kim Jong-Kook made a name for himself as a solo artist and TV personality, Turbo reunited as a trio with Kim Jong-Kook, Kim Jung-Nam, and Mikey. They released a comeback album on December 21, 2015 titled *Again*.

TVXQ

TVXQ is an S.M. Entertainment group that debuted in 2003. The original members of the group were U-Know Yunho, Max Changmin, Hero Jaejoong, Micky Yoochun, and Xiah Junsu. They released their first song, "Hug," in January of 2004 and they almost immediately became stars. They released their first studio album shortly after, *Tri-Angle*, which became a best-seller. In September of 2005, they released their second studio album, *Rising Sun*, and it was met with the same success as their first album.

During this time, TVXQ was also gaining a lot of popularity in Japan as they released several singles and also appeared on some shows. By March of 2006, the group had released their fourth Japanese single and in 2006, they embarked on their first concert tour of Japan from May to June.

In 2009, TVXQ fans shook their fandom as Jaejoong, Yoochun, and Junsu left the group and signed with C-JeS Entertainment. There was a long legal battle between the three members and their former agency, but the trio eventually started their own group and in April of 2010, made their record debut in Japan. Yunho and Changmin made their return as a duo with the album *Keep Your Head Down* on January 5, 2011. Yunho and Changmin still continue to promote as TVXQ today. They released their eighth studio album, *New Chapter #1: The Chance of Love*, on March 28, 2018.

TWICE

TWICE is a girl group that was formed under JYP Entertainment in 2015. There are nine members in the group who are: Nayeon, Jeongyeon, Momo, Sana, Jihyo, Mina, Dahyun, Chaeyoung, and Tzuyu. Their EP, *The Story Begins*, and song, "Like Ooh-Ahh," were released on October 20, 2015. Their second EP, *Page Two*, was released on April 25, 2016. The song they promoted was "Cheer Up" and it reached number one on the charts and music programs pretty easily. On October 24, 2017, their music video for the song "TWICE" was released online.

By the end of 2017, TWICE's song "Cheer Up" won Song of the Year at the 8th Melon Music Awards and 18th Mnet Asian Music Awards.

2AM

2AM is a boy group that formed under JYP Entertainment. The members are Jo Kwon, Lee Changmin, Lim Seulong, and Jeong Jinwoon. The group debuted with "This Song" in July of 2008. They released another single in March of 2009, "Confession of a Friend." In January of 2010, the group released their EP, *Even If I Die I Can't Let You Go.*

The group is known for their romantic ballads and smooth vocals. As a result, they've won many prestigious awards, including the Digital Bonsang Award in 2010 at the Golden Disc Awards, Best Vocal Performance—Group Award at the Mnet Asian Music Awards in 2010, Song of the Year Award at the Melon Music Awards in 2010, and the Bonsang Award at the Seoul Music Awards in 2011.

2 Days & 1 Night

2 Days & 1 Night is a variety show that showcases a group of cast members embarking on an overnight trip. The current cast members are Kim Jong-Min, Cha Tae-Hyun, Kim Joon-Ho, Defconn, Jung Joon-Young, and Yoon Shi-Yoon. There are various missions, games, and obstacles that the members have to complete throughout the two days. Most of the time, if the members fail to win or complete a task, they are unable to eat. There are also various K-pop idols or celebrities who appear on the show.

2PM

2PM is a boy group that was formed under JYP Entertainment in 2008. The original members of the group were Jun. K, Nickhun,

Taecyeon, Wooyoung, Junho, Chansung, and Jay Park. The group debuted with the song "10 Out of 10" on September 4, 2008, which was a huge success. On April 2009, they released their second mini-album, *2:00PM Time For Change*.

Later in 2009, the leader of the group, Jay Park, was involved in a scandal in the midst of the release of the group's first studio album, *01:59PM*. Despite the scandal, the group won the award for Best Male group and Artist of the Year at the Mnet Asian Music Awards. It was announced in February 2010 that Jay Park would not be returning to the group.

The success of 2PM has not ceased. They released five more albums in Korea and five albums in Japan. They've won several awards, not only in Korea but also in Japan, which have included Best Album of the Year at the Japan Gold Disc Awards in 2016, Best Group Video (2012) and Best Album of the Year (2013) at the MTV Video Music Awards Japan.

Two Yoo Project—Sugar Man

Two Yoo Project—Sugar Man is a music show that first aired in 2015. Yoo Jae-Suk and Yoo Hee-Yeol are the two main hosts of the show. It involves veteran artists from the past coming on the show and singing their past hit songs. New K-pop groups, idols, or artists sing covers of the songs with their own twist on it and the audience votes on which version they like best.

Uh-kkang

The term used to refer to a male who has broad shoulders.
E.g., "Did you see Rain's shoulders? They're so broad!"
"For real, he's seriously uh-kkang!"

U-KISS

U-Kiss is a boy group that was formed by NH Media in 2008. Their name stands for "Ubiquitous Korean-International Idol Super Star." The original six members in the group were Alexander, Kim Kibum, Dongho, Kevin, Soohyun, and Eli. The group debuted in Japan in August of 2018 and debuted in Korea with their mini-album titled *New Generation*. Their second mini-album was titled *Bring It Back 2 Old School*, which they released in 2009 and their song, "I Like You," was quite popular in Thailand.

Alexander and Kibum left the group in 2011 and AJ and Hoon joined the lineup. With the new members, they released their fifth mini-album, *Brand New Kiss*.

In August of 2016, AJ's contract expired with the agency and he left the group. In March of 2017, Kevin also left the group as his contract had expired. Soohyun, Kiseop, Eli, Hoon, and Jun remain in the group.

Ultimate Bias

Ultimate bias refers to a fan's all-time favorite singer or artist. This person is on the top of their list of favorite artists, singers, or celebrities.

E.g., "My ultimate bias is Lee Dong-Hae from Super Junior."

Ulzzang

The term "ulzzang" refers to someone who has a very attractive face. "Ul" is short for "Ul-gool" in Korean, which means "face" and "zzang" means "the best." It was originally an online competition, but now it has become a general term that refers to people who are very good-looking.

E.g., "Jung Yong Hwa is SOOOO good-looking!"

"I agree. Did you know he was named ulzzang when he was in high school?!"

"I can see why!"

Um Jung-Hwa

Um Jung-Hwa was born on August 17, 1969. Her career started in the early '90s when she released her first album, *Sorrowful Secret*. She was a successful female artist and paved the way for a lot of other solo female artists and K-pop groups. She had a plethora of hits that are considered classics today. Some of these songs include

"Sad Expectation," "A Love Only Heaven Permits," and the Jinusean song she was featured in, "Tell Me."

In the 2000s, Um Jung-Hwa took an interest in acting and has since become one of the top actresses in the industry. She has won several awards for her roles including Best Actress at the 7th Busan Film Critics Awards for her role in *Princess Aurora*, Best Actress at the 48th Paeksang Arts Awards for her role in *Dancing Queen*, and the Best Actress at the 50th Grand Bell Awards for her film *Montage*.

Um-Chin-Ah

Um-Chin-Ah is the slang term that refers to a son who is very close to his mother. It's a shortened acronym for the sentence, "mom's friend and son" in Korean.

Um-Chin-Ddal

Um-chin-ddal is the slang term that refers to a daughter who is very close to her mother. The "um" is a short version of the word "mom" in Korean; the "chin" is short for "chin-goo," which means "friend" in Korean; and the "ddal" part of the acronym means "daughter."

UNB

UNB is a boy group that was formed as a result of the singing reality show called *The Unit*. The members include Marco, Go Ho-Jung, Ji Han-Sol, Jun, Euijin, Feeldog, Daewon, Chan, and Kijung. The group made their debut with the release of their EP, *Boyhood*, on

April 7, 2018. They promoted the songs "Feeling" and "ONLY ONE" off their first EP. Their second EP was released on June 28, 2018, which was titled B*lack Heart*.

UNI.T

UNI.T is a girl group that was formed on the reality singing show The Unit. They were the nine girls who made it to the final round to form the girl group. The members are Yang Ji-Won, Woohee, Yoonjo, ZN, NC.A, Euijin, Yebin, Lee Hyun-Joo, and Lee Su-Ji. The group released their first EP, *Line*, on May 18, 2018. They promoted the song "No More" and their official stage debut was on the music program *Music Bank*.

UNIQ

UNIQ was formed in 2014 under Yuehua Entertainment. They are a five-member group that has members from both China and Korea. The members include Zhou Yixuan, Kim Sungjoo, Li Wenhan, Cho Seungyoun, and Wang Yibo. The group had their stage debut on the music program *M Countdown* on October 16, 2014. A few days later, they released their single, "Falling In Love," in both China and South Korea. On November 25, 2014, the group made their debut in China. Their first mini-album, titled *EOEO*, was released on April 6, 2015. They promoted the title track for their album, which was also called "EOEO."

The Unit

The Unit is an audition-based singing reality show that results in two final groups: one boy group of nine members and one girl group of nine members. Only one season aired, beginning on October 28, 2017. The last episode of the season was on February 10, 2018. The result of the show was the formation of the boy group UNB and girl group UNI.T.

United Cube

United Cube is what all the artists under Cube Entertainment are called.

United Cube Concert

In 2013, Cube Entertainment's artists, including Beast, 4Minute, BtoB, and G.NA, performed at the United Cube Concert. After five years, the agency announced that they will be having another United Cube concert on June 16, 2018. The lineup included HyunA, Jo Kwon, BtoB, CLC, Pentagon, and (G)I-DLE. There must have been a lot of anticipation and excitement for this concert as tickets were sold out within two minutes!

Unnie

Unnie is the term used from a younger female who is referring to an older female. It is a term used when the two girls are in a close and comfortable relationship with each other. It is also used when the sisters are blood related.

Unnies

Unnies is a group that was formed as a result of the show *Sister's Slam Dunk*. There were two seasons of the show and two groups with slightly different members. In the first season, the members of Unnies were Ra Mi-Ran, Kim Sook, Hong Jin-Kyung, Min Hyo-Rin, Jessi, and Tiffany. They released a song titled "Shut Up" that was produced by Park Jin-young (JYP Entertainment). The second season of "Unnies" included celebrities Kim Sook, Hong Jin-Kyung, Kang Ye-Won, Han Chae-Young, Hong Jin-Young, Minzy, and Jeon So-Mi.

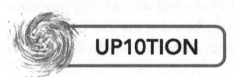

UP10TION

UP10TION was formed in 2015 by TOP Media. The members are Jinhoo, Kuhn, Kogyeol, Wei, Bitto, Wooshin, Sunyoul, Gyujin, Hwanhee, and Xiao. On September 11, 2015, they released their mini-album titled *Top Secret* and their single, "So Dangerous."

Uptown

Uptown is a hip-hop group that was prominent in the mid '90s. The original members were Chris Jung, Carlos Galvan, Steve Kim, and Tasha. The group went through some member changes when Jung, Galvan, Kim, and Reid left the group. Jessica H.O, Maniac, Snacky Chan, and Swings joined as new members. They released an album in 2009 titled *New Era* and an album in 2010 titled *Surprise*.

Urban Zakapa

Urban Zakapa is a co-ed R&B group that was formed in 2009. They were signed under Fluxus Entertainment and were originally a nine-member group. The original members were Park Yong-In, Jo Hyun-Ah, Kwon Sun-Il, Choi Jae-Man, Yoon Ji-Min, Choi Yoon-Jeong, Lee Ji-Ho, Baek Ha Kyoung Ki, and Han Tae-Young. In 2009, the group released their first two EPs and in 2011, they released their first album, *01*.

In 2012, the group became a trio with members Park Yong-In, Jo Hyun-Ah, and Kwon Sun-Il. On April 3, 2012, the trio released their third EP, "Beautiful Day." The group released three more albums in 2012, 2013, and 2014 and on February 19, 2016, they signed with a new agency, MakeUs Entertainment. Their success grew and they became even more recognized in the industry as they won two awards in 2017: the Digital Bonsang Award at the 31st Golden Disk Awards and the Song of the Month Award at the 6th Gaon Chart Music Awards.

V-Line

V-Line is a term that refers to an idol's face being shaped like a V. It is considered beautiful to have a sharp and pointy chin with a small face. A prime example of a K-pop idol with the V-line is Davichi's Kang Minkyung.

V Live

V Live is a live streaming service where fans can catch live interviews and other promotional videos of their favorite K-pop idols and celebrities. Fans can leave live comments while they watch live footage of their favorite idols. It's a great platform where celebrities can interact with their fans and respond to questions or comments.

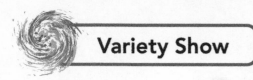

Variety Show

Variety show is a genre of a television program that exhibits many random elements in one program. There is often a host and a cast that do random things on the show, including dancing, singing, playing games, and generally just being funny. Some of the most successful variety shows have been *X-Man*, where they invite lots of K-pop idols or celebrities to play several mini games on the show against each other; *Infinite Challenge*, in which the cast members would have to take on crazy challenges every week; and *Running Man*, where the cast members and guests would have to complete crazy obstacles and challenges in order to win at the end!

VAV

VAV, which stands for "Very Awesome Voice," is a boy group that was formed in 2015 by A Team Entertainment. The current members are St.Van, Baron, ACE, Ayno, Jacob, Lou, and Ziu. They debuted with their EP titled *Under The Moonlight* in November of 2015.

Victon

Victon is a boy group that was formed under the label Plan A Entertainment. The members of the group are Choi Byung-Chan, Do Han-Se, Jung Su-Bin, Heo Chan, Lim Se-Jun, Han Seung-Woo, and Kang Seung-Sik. Their first EP, *Voice to New World*, was released on November 9, 2016. They promoted their first single, which was called "I'm Fine."

V.I.P

V.I.P is the name given to BIGBANG fans. Meaning "very important person," it shows how important BIGBANG's fandom is to them!

Visual

Visual is the term used to describe a member in a K-pop group who is the "best-looking." There are often roles that are given to each member and "visual" is one of them.

E.g., Friend 1: "I love Moonbin from Astro! He's the best-looking in the group by far!"

Friend 2: "He is handsome, but Eunwoo is the visual! He's so dreamy!"

VIXX

VIXX is a boy group that was formed in 2012 under Jellyfish Entertainment. Their name stands for "Voice, Visual, Value in Excelsis." The members of VIXX include N, Leo, Ken, Ravi, Hongbin, and Hyuk. Fans were familiar with the VIXX members even before their debut as all of the members were contestants on the reality show *MyDOL*.

The members made their debut as a group on May 24, 2012 on the music program *M Countdown*, while performing their single, "Super Hero." Their second single was released on August 14, "Rock Ur Body." The first album they released was on November 25, 2013, called *Voodoo*, and they promoted the song "Voodoo Doll." Their success was evident as they were able to win first place on the music program *Music Bank* that same week. Since then,

VIXX has gone on to release three more studio albums: *Chained Up* (2015), *Eau de VIXX* (2018), and a Japanese album, *Depend on Me* (2016).

With their success, VIXX has won twenty-six awards, including the Disc Bonsang Award for three years in a row at the Golden Disk Awards in 2015, 2016, and 2017.

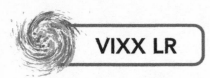

VIXX LR

VIXX LR is a sub-unit group of VIXX. The sub-unit was formed in August of 2015 with the members Leo and Ravi. The "LR" in their group name represents their names. They've also mentioned that the "LR" can stand for "left" and "right" in that they have contrasting qualities on stage. The sub-unit debuted with the mini-album, *Beautiful Liar* on August 17, 2015. They proved to be successful as they were nominated for two awards at the 2015 Mnet Asian Music Awards and won the Best Sub-unit/Collaboration Awards at the KMC Radio Awards.

Voisper

Voisper is a group that was formed in January of 2015 under Evermore Music. Their name is a combination of the two words "voice" and "whisper." The group members are Jung Dae-Gwang, Jung Kwang-Ho, Kim Kang-San, and Min Chung-Ki. The group debuted on February 16, 2016, by appearing on *The Show*, performing "In Your Voice."

Wanna One

Wanna One is an eleven-member boy group that was formed as a result of the second season of the competition show *Produce 101*. The group members are Yoon Ji-Sung, Ha Sung-Woon, Hwang Min-Hyun, Ong Seong-Wu, Kim Jae-Hwan, Kang Daniel, Park Ji-Hoon, Park Woo-Jin, Bae Jin-Young, Lee Dae-Hwi, and Lai Guan-Lin.

There were 101 contestants and the final eleven made the group Wanna One. The group signed with YMC Entertainment upon winning and debuted on August 7, 2017, releasing their EP titled *1x1=1 (To Be One)* the following day. They promoted the title track, "Energetic," which became a huge success.

In the summer of 2018, starting in June, Wanna One embarked on their first world tour, called Wanna One World Tour, One: The World. On June 1, Swing Entertainment became the agency for Wanna One.

Wanna One has proven to be a huge success in the K-pop world as the group was chosen by its fans. They've sold millions of albums and although their time together is limited, they have left a big mark in the K-pop world. Their success has spoken volumes as they have even won some big awards, including New Artist of the Year at the Golden Disc Awards (2018), Best New Artist at the Melon Music Awards (2017), Best New Male Artist and Best Male Group at the Mnet Asian Music Awards (2017), and the Bonsang and New Artist Award at the Seoul Music Awards (2018).

Wassup

Wassup is a girl group that is signed under Sony Music. The original members of the group were Dain, Jinju, Nada, Nari, Jiae, Sujin, and Woojoo. The group debuted with a music video for the song "Wassup," and on November 20, 2013, they released their EP titled *Nom Nom Nom*. Wassup became even more well-known when they released their music video for the song "Fire" in June of 2014. The music video was released to celebrate the 2014 FIFA World Cup.

On February of 2017, it was announced that Nada had left the group and Dain and Jinju were in the process of suing their company. The remaining four members were Nari, Jiae, Sujin, and Woojoo. They continued to promote as a group and they released their third mini-album, titled *ColorTV*, in April 2017.

We Got Married

We Got Married is an MBC reality show that aired from 2008 to 2017. The premise of the show was to bring celebrities together in a mock wedding and to follow their pretend marriage for a certain amount of time. There have been a lot of popular K-pop idols who have partaken in the show, including Super Junior's Leeteuk, SHINee's Lee Tae-Min, CNBLUE's Jung Yong-Hwa and Lee Jong-Hyun, MAMAMOO's Solar, BtoB's Yook Sung Jae, and Apink's Son Na-Eun.

Weekly Idol

Weekly Idol is a popular variety show that started in 2011. The show was originally hosted by Jeong Hyung-Don and Defconn, who have since been replaced with Lee Sang-Min, Yoo Se-Yoon, and Kim Shin-Young. It is a popular show featuring K-pop groups and artists every week. They play hilarious games and have fun interviews that K-pop fans love.

Weki Meki

Weki Meki is a girl group that was formed in 2017 under Fantagio. There are eight members in the group: Suyeon, Elly, Yoojung, Doyeon, Sei, Lua, Rina, and Lucy. Prior to their debut, Elly, Yoojung, Doyeon, and Sei participated in the reality K-pop show *Produce 101*. Yoojung and Doyeon were two of the final eleven members who were part of the project group I.O.I.

They released their debut EP, *WEME*, in August of 2017, along with the single "I Don't Like Your Girlfriend." In February of 2018, they released their second EP, *Lucky*, with the singles "La La La" and "Butterfly."

Wheesung

Wheesung was born on February 5, 1982. He is best known for being an R&B singer who was signed under M Boat, a company that was affiliated with YG Entertainment. He debuted in 2002 with the album *Like a Movie*, and then released *It's Real* in 2003. His singles became instant successes and he became a bestselling artist. In 2006, Wheesung left YG and signed with Orange Shock

Agency. In June of 2009, Wheesung again signed with a new label, POP/UP Entertainment, which led to him transferring to YMC Entertainment in 2011. Although he has not been as active since then, Wheesung has completed his military duties and started his own agency called Realslow.

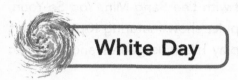

White Day

In South Korea, Valentine's Day (February 14) is a day where the women usually give chocolates and candies to men. White Day takes place on March and is a day where the men gift women with chocolates/candies, flowers, and/or stuffed animals.

E.g., Friend 1: "Are you getting your girlfriend anything for White Day?!"

Friend 2: "Of course! I'm going to get her some chocolates and candy. She got me chocolates on Valentine's Day."

Winner

Winner is a group that was formed under YG Entertainment in 2013. The original members of the group were Jinwoo, Seunghoon, Mino, Seungyoon, and Taehyun, but Taehyun departed from the group in 2016. The group was formed as a result of the reality show called *WIN: Who Is Next*.

Winner had a debut showcase on August 6, 2014, and they released their album, *2014 S/S*, on August 12. They won first place on the music program *M Countdown*, which showed the group's promising potential as a K-pop group. Their song, "Empty," reached all-kill status, which was a huge feat considering the group had just debuted.

In 2015, the group embarked on some solo activities. Taehyun, Seungyoon, and Jinwoo did some acting, while Mino made it to the final two in the popular Mnet rap show *Show Me the Money.* In February of 2016, Winner released a mini-album titled *EXIT:E,* with singles "Baby Baby" and "Sentimental" topping the charts. On April 4, 2018, the group released their second studio album, *EVERYD4Y.*

Wonder Girls

Wonder Girls was the popular girl group formed by JYP Entertainment in 2007. The original members of the group were Yeeun, Sunye, Sunmi, Hyuna, Sohee, and Hyelim, but Hyuna departed from the group later in 2007 and was replaced by Yubin shortly after. Further changes to the lineup involved Sunmi leaving the group in 2010 and Sunye leaving in 2014. The four members Yeeun, Yubin, Sunmi, and Hyerim continued to promote as a four-member group until their disbandment in 2017.

Wonder Girls made their official debut on the music program *Show! Music Core* in 2007, performing their song, "Irony," from their first album, *The Wonder Years.* The success of Wonder Girls didn't seem to stop, as they won some prestigious awards early on in their career, including Digital Bonsang, Popularity Award at the Golden Disc Awards in 2007, Best New Artist at the Seoul Music Awards in 2007, the Bonsang and Daesang Award in 2009, and the Best Female Group, Song of the Year, and Best Music Video Awards at the Mnet Asian Music Awards in 2008, to name a few.

In 2009, the group was chosen to be the opening act for the Jonas Brothers, singing their song "Nobody" in English. They even reached the Billboard Hot 100 Chart, making them the first K-pop group in South Korea to do this, which was a huge feat.

X-Man

X-Man was a popular variety show that aired from 2003 to 2007 on SBS. It was originally hosted by Yoo Jae-Suk, Kang Ho-Dong, and Kim Je-Dong, but Kim Je-Dong got replaced in 2004. It was a program that invited popular K-pop idols and celebrities on the show where they would play a lot of creative and funny games against each other. It was popular mainly for the entertaining hosts, the quirky and fun games, and the stars that would make guest appearances.

Yang Hyun-Suk

Yang Hyun-Suk is the CEO of YG Entertainment, one of the most
successful entertainment agencies in South Korea. Before he
became a CEO, he was a dancer and rapper. He was originally a
member of the group Seo Taiji and Boys in the '90s, which made
him very famous across the nation.

In 1998, he started his agency, YG Entertainment, and produced
music for a lot of K-pop groups that were popular in the '90s and
2000s. He was also a judge on the popular reality singing show
K-Pop Star, where he met and signed some of his current artists.

Yangpa

Yangpa (otherwise known as Lee Eun-Jin) is a singer who was most
popular for her ballads and high-ranged vocals in the '90s. She
released her first studio album in 1996, titled *Grasshopper's Love*,
and promoted the song with the same title. She became almost an
instant success. She went on to make four more studio albums and
even won the Best Ballad Performance Award at the Mnet Asian
Music Awards in 2007. Although she hasn't really been in the

public eye that much, Yangpa has made several appearances on various variety shows, like *Immortal Song 2* in 2016.

YG Entertainment

In 1996, YG Entertainment (YG) was founded by Yang Hyun Suk (former Seo Taijji and Boys member) and his little brother, Yang Min Suk. YG is considered to be one of the most successful and wildly popular talent agencies in all of South Korea. Despite what most people may think, YG not only produces some of K-pop's most successful groups and singers, but also contracts models, actors, and producers.

Since its beginning, YG's success has been on full display by signing popular K-pop groups and artists, including 1TYM, 2NE1, and PSY. The agency is currently home to many internationally known K-pop groups and artists like BIGBANG, Akdong Musician, Winner, iKon, Sechskies, BLACKPINK, Lee Hi, CL, and Dara.

Yim Jae-Beom

Yim Jae-Beom is a famous rock ballad singer who used to sing for the group Sinawe in the '80s. After he left the group, he became a solo artist and became popular for a lot of his singles like "For You," "Confession," and "Scars Deeper Than Love," which are covered quite often by K-pop idols and celebrities on variety shows.

Yoo Hee-Yeol

Yoo Hee-Yeol was born on April 19, 1971 in Seoul, South Korea. He is popular for starting the band Toy in 1994 alongside Yoon

Jeong-Oh. After the release of their first album, Yoo Hee-Yeol left the group to study and to complete his mandatory military service. When he returned to Toy in 1996, Yoo Hee-Yeol was the only member in the group and still released a second album. His song "Remember I Was Next To You" was a huge hit. Since then, he has produced songs for many famous names in the music industry, like Lee Seung-Hwan, Yoon Jong-Shin, and Lee Moon-Se.

In 1997, he founded Antenna Music, a recording company. Yoo Hee-Yeol has also been active on several variety shows including his own show, *Yoo Hee-Yeol's Sketchbook*.

Yoo Hee-Yeol's Sketchbook

Yoo Hee-Yeol's Sketchbook is a music program that started in 2009. It airs every Friday and is hosted by singer Yoo Hee-Yeol. The program involves music guests coming on the show and performing their songs, as well as engaging in a short interview with the host. There are a lot of K-pop artists and idols who appear on the show including some of the most respected artists in the industry.

Yoo Seung-Joon

Yoo Seung-Joon was born on December 15, 1976. He is a Korean American who became a popular a K-pop singer in the '90s. He debuted in 1997 with the album *West Side* and became popular for his title track, "Nightmare." He released another album in 1998, *1998 V2 for SALE*, and promoted the song "Na Na Na," which also became a huge success. His third album, *Now or Never*, was released in 1999. Since then, he has released four more albums, most of which have dominated the charts.

In 2002, Yoo was deported back to the US as a result of becoming a US citizen, which meant he was unable to fulfill his mandatory military service in Korea. He left Seoul and was not allowed to return.

Yoo Young-Jin

Yoo Young-Jin is a well-known producer in the K-pop industry under S.M. Entertainment. He produced songs for the legendary K-pop group H.O.T back in the '90s and has continued to produce megahits for a lot of the K-pop groups that are dominating the charts today. Some of the hit songs he's produced are H.O.T's "We Are the Future," S.E.S's "I'm Your Girl," BoA's "ID; Peace B," Shinhwa's "Hey, Come On!," TVXQ's "Rising Sun," Super Junior's "Sorry, Sorry," SHINee's "Ring Ding Dong," and EXO's "Mama"—to name a few!

Yoon Do-Hyun

Yoon Do-Hyun was born on February 3, 1972, and he is best known for being the frontman for his band, Yoon Do-Hyun Band. He's a rock singer and songwriter and has been in the music industry since the mid '90s.

Yoon Jong-Shin

Yoon Jong-Shin was born on October 15, 1969, and is a singer-songwriter, producer, and TV show host. He also founded an entertainment agency called Mystic Entertainment in 2001. Yoon Jong-Shin has been in the music industry since 1991, when he released his first album, titled *Like the First Time We Met*. Since then, he has released eighteen more albums and has also made a name for himself in the variety show world. He was on the shows *Secretly Greatly*, *Family Outing*, and *Heart Signal*, and is currently a host on the show *Radio Star*.

Yoon Mi-Rae

Yoon Mi-Rae was born on May 31, 1981. She is best known for being in the '90s hip-hop group Uptown. In 2001, she released her first solo album, *As Time Goes By*. People took to Yoon Mi-Rae for her ability to both rap and sing. She released three more albums as a solo artist, which were *Gemini* (May 3, 2002), *To My Love* (December 5, 2002), and *Yoonmirae* (February 23, 2007).

In 2013, she formed a hip-hop trio called MFBTY (My Fans Better Than Yours) with rappers Tiger JK and Bizzy. The trio signed onto Tiger JK's label, Ghood Music, that same year.

Younha

Younha, otherwise known as Go Yun-Ha, was born on April 29, 1988. She is a singer and a producer. Younha started her career in Japan in 2004 when she released her single, "Yubikiri." Her second single was released in Japan, "Houkiboshi," which is the song that gained her a lot of success. After the release of two more singles, she released her first album, titled *Go! Younha*.

In 2006, Younha debuted in Korea with the single *Audition*, and in 2007, she released her first album, *The Perfect Day to Say I Love You*, which was a big success. She even won the Best New Artist Award at the Mnet Asian Music Awards in 2007 for the song "Password 486" off her album. Since her first album, Younha has released six more albums and has made her mark in the music industry as being one of the best singer-songwriters.

ZE:A

ZE:A is a boy group that was formed in 2010 under Star Empire Entertainment. The members of the group are Kevin, Hwang Kwang-Hee, Park Hyung-Sik, Im Si-Wan, Moon Jun-Young, Kim Tae-Heon, Jung Hee-Chul, Ha Min-Woo, and Kim Dong-Jun. On January 7, 2010, the group came out with their single album, titled *Nativity*. A few months later, on March 25, 2010, they released another single album, *Leap for Detonation*, promoting the title track "All Day Long."

Their first full-length album, *Lovability*, was released on March 17, 2011, and their second album was released in 2012, titled *Spectacular*. Although the group was quite successful in the K-pop world, several of the group members have gone on to become well-known actors. Im Si-Wan has been praised for his role in several dramas including *Moon Embracing the Sun*, *Misaeng*, and the hit film *The Attorney*. Park Hyung-Sik has starred in several K-dramas as well: *Hwarang*, *Strong Woman Do Bong Soon*, and *Suits*. Kim Dong-Jun has been in several films and K-dramas, including *A Company Man*, *Dead Again*, *Black*, and *About Time*. The members have not only left an impression on the K-drama world, but ZE:A member Hwang Kwang-Hee has made quite the name for himself appearing on a lot of the most popular shows, including *We Got Married*, *Law of the Jungle*, and *Infinite Challenge*.

ZE:A's

On July of 2010, ZE:A officially named their fandom ZE:A's which means ZE:A STYLE.

Zico

Zico is a rapper, producer, and leader of the boy group Block B. In November of 2014, Zico released his first solo debut single, "Tough Cookie." His second single followed on February 13, 2015, which was titled "Well Done."

In May 2015, Zico was chosen as a producer for the popular show *Show Me the Money* 4. He produced several songs for his team of rappers, which included "Turtle Song," "Moneyflow," and "Fear."

In November of 2015, Zico released his first EP as a solo artist, *EP*, with the title track "Eureka." The song was an instant hit and was noted for its catchy melody and lyrics. Zico's success as a producer didn't stop here as he produced a song for Kim Se-Jeong on the show *Talents for Sale*, which topped various charts.

Zico's success as a producer has won him several awards, including Best Male Artist at the Mnet Asian Music Awards (2016), Digital Bonsang Award at the 31st Golden Disc Awards (2017), and the Bonsang Award at the 26th Seoul Music Awards (2017).

Zion.T

Zion.T, whose real name is Kim Hae-Sol, was born on April 13, 1989. He is an R&B singer who was originally with the label Amoeba Culture, but then he moved to The Black Label in 2016.

On April 9, 2013, Zion.T released his first album, *Red Light*, which was a big success. He won the Best R&B & Soul Album for it at the 11th Korean Music Awards. In December of the same year, he released an EP titled *Mirrorball*. In 2015, Zion.T collaborated with many artists like Crush, Jonghyun, and PSY, and released several singles that were chart-toppers. He won two awards that year at the Mnet Asian Music Awards: Best Vocal Performance—Male and Best Collaboration & Unit.